Barry Sanders

FOOTBALL ⬤ SUPERSTARS

Tiki Barber

Tom Brady

John Elway

Brett Favre

Peyton Manning

Dan Marino

Donovan McNabb

Joe Montana

Walter Payton

Jerry Rice

Ben Roethlisberger

Barry Sanders

FOOTBALL ● SUPERSTARS

Barry Sanders

Samuel Willard Crompton

CHELSEA HOUSE
PUBLISHERS
An imprint of Infobase Publishing

BARRY SANDERS

Copyright © 2008 by Infobase Publishing

All rights reserved. No part of this book may be reproduced or utilized in any form or by any means, electronic or mechanical, including photocopying, recording, or by any information storage or retrieval systems, without permission in writing from the publisher. For information, contact:

Chelsea House
An imprint of Infobase Publishing
132 West 31st Street
New York NY 10001

Library of Congress Cataloging-in-Publication Data
Crompton, Samuel Willard.
 Barry Sanders / Samuel Willard Crompton.
   p. cm. -- (Football superstars)
 Includes bibliographical references and index.
 ISBN 978-0-7910-9667-3 (hardcover)
 1. Sanders, Barry, 1968---Juvenile literature. 2. Football players--United States--Biography--Juvenile literature. I. Title. II. Series.

 GV939.S18C76 2008
 796.332092--dc22
 [B]

                    2008005763

Chelsea House books are available at special discounts when purchased in bulk quantities for businesses, associations, institutions, or sales promotions. Please call our Special Sales Department in New York at (212) 967-8800 or (800) 322-8755.

You can find Chelsea House on the World Wide Web at http://www.chelseahouse.com

Text design by Erik Lindstrom
Composition by EJB Publishing Services
Cover design by Ben Peterson
Cover printed by Yurchak Printing, Landisville, Pa.
Book printed and bound by Yurchak Printing, Landisville, Pa.
Printed in the United States of America

This book is printed on acid-free paper.

All links and Web addresses were checked and verified to be correct at the time of publication. Because of the dynamic nature of the Web, some addresses and links may have changed since publication and may no longer be valid.

CONTENTS

Cowboys' Battle

People take sports way too seriously.

—Barry Sanders

Two teams with the same nickname clashed at the 1988 Holiday Bowl, with a spectacular **running back** winning most of the applause. Observers—whether amateur or professional—declared that December 30, 1988, marked the full-blown arrival of a new phenom in sport: a running back who seemingly could not be stopped.

Founded in 1886, the University of Wyoming fielded its first football team seven years later. It's hard to say when Wyoming first called its players "Cowboys," but the name endures today. Wyoming fans take Cowboy football so seriously that on game days War Memorial Stadium, with a capacity of 33,500, becomes the third-largest city in the state. (Wyoming perennially comes in last or next-to-last in population of the 50 states.)

Established in 1890, Oklahoma State University (OSU) played its first football game in 1901. Wearing orange and black, the OSU Cowboys became a regular feature in Big Eight college football. No one called the OSU Cowboys "copycats" for their nickname, for it made sense that two frontier teams, one from the Great Plains and the other from the Rocky Mountains, would adopt such a moniker.

With each having stellar seasons, the OSU Cowboys and the Wyoming Cowboys earned their way to a meeting in sunny San Diego, California, at the end of 1988.

WYOMING'S 1988 SEASON

The Wyoming Cowboys began their 1988 season by playing the Brigham Young Cougars at home. Wyoming got off to a great start, thrashing the Cougars, 24-14, in an upset that won the team national attention. Wyoming went on to beat Louisville (at Louisville), 44-9; Louisiana Tech at home, 38-6; and Air Force (at Air Force) in a wild 48-45 shootout, one of the highest-scoring games of the entire college season. Wyoming won the game with a **field goal** in the last second of play. By now, Wyoming had one of the top-scoring offensive units in the nation, led by **quarterback** Randy Welniak, and it entered the Top 20 poll for the first time that year.

Wyoming then beat Fullerton State at home, 35-16; San Diego State at San Diego, 55-27; and New Mexico at home by a ripping 55-7 score. Their record of seven victories and no defeats had the Wyoming Cowboys at or near the eleventh spot in most national polls, a ranking not seen since the glory days of coach Lloyd Eaton, who had won two-thirds of his games from 1962 to 1970.

The Wyoming Cowboys beat Utah in a home game, 61-18, then thrashed archrival Colorado State (both squads claimed to be the *real* Rocky Mountain team), 48-14, in a road game. Early in November, Wyoming obliterated Texas-El Paso 51-6 at home, but the following week the Cowboys lost their attempt at a perfect season, with a 34-10 defeat at the University of Houston.

Perhaps it was the pressure of an undefeated record; maybe it was a letdown after 10 spectacular weeks. Whatever the reason, Welniak was sacked five times in the first quarter, four times in the second, and by game's end he had bitten the dust a total of 16 times. "Our pride is hurt," he told the writers of *Sports Illustrated*.

There was one last regular-season game, one played neither in the Rocky Mountains nor on the Great Plains. The Wyoming Cowboys beat the Hawaii Rainbow Warriors 28-22 at Aloha Stadium to end their season with a feeling of triumph. Even so, the single loss to Houston on November 12 had hurt the team's standing: Wyoming slipped from ninth to seventeenth in most college football polls.

OKLAHOMA STATE'S 1988 SEASON

The OSU Cowboys came into the 1988 season with confidence, and for good reason. Under coach Pat Jones, they had gone 10–2 the previous year and had prevailed over West Virginia, 35-33, in the Sun Bowl. OSU played its first 1988 game at home, against the Miami (Ohio) RedHawks.

Some observers felt that OSU would be at a disadvantage because of the loss of running back Thurman Thomas to the pros: He had been drafted by the Buffalo Bills that spring. For the previous two years, Thomas had been backed up by **wingback** Barry Sanders, perceived as a fine back but not as good as Thomas. Sanders took the opening **kickoff** from the RedHawks and ran 100 **yards**, all the way down the field, for six points. (He had done the same against the Tulsa Golden Hurricane the year before and remains the only college player ever to have returned two consecutive year-opening kickoffs for **touchdowns**.)

Those who watched Sanders on September 10, and for the rest of the season, came to admire his terrific running style. He

Barry Sanders sprinted toward the end zone on a 58-yard run in a game between Oklahoma State and Texas Tech played on December 4, 1988, in Tokyo, Japan. Sanders's outstanding season led Oklahoma State to a 9–2 regular-season record. In this game, the season finale, Sanders rushed for 257 yards and scored four touchdowns.

used his legs as well as any man—maybe better—but he was also adroit at using his lungs: darting in and out from defenders, finding an opening, and going as far down the field as he could. His admirers, and they were many, also pointed to his lack of histrionics: He never spiked a ball or questioned a referee's decision. Then again he seldom needed to; his performance spoke for itself.

With quarterback Mike Gundy throwing well and with Sanders running the ball and forcing the issue, OSU had a banner season. The OSU Cowboys beat Texas A&M at home, 52-15, Tulsa at home, 56-35, and slapped Colorado (at

Colorado), 41-21, before being taken down by Nebraska, at Nebraska, 63-42. OSU resumed its winning ways by beating Missouri 49-21, and Kansas State 45-27, but the Cowboys lost at home to their all-time rival, the University of Oklahoma, 31-28. OSU ended its season by beating Kansas 63-24, and Iowa State 49-28, and then the team traveled all the way to Tokyo, Japan, to play Texas Tech. In that final game of the season, Sanders carried the ball 42 times (a personal record for his college career), gained 257 yards, and ran for four touchdowns as OSU slipped by Texas Tech 45-42. By now, experts pointed out that Sanders had scored at least two touchdowns in *every single game* he had played in 1988. Some thought that his 1988 performance was one of the best of any single college year; some thought it was *the* best.

THE HEISMAN

Sanders was in Tokyo when he heard the news: He was the **Heisman Trophy** winner for 1988.

Most people who knew Sanders believed that he put too little energy into self-promotion. When he learned that the Heisman Trophy winner would be announced while he was in Tokyo, Sanders practically grimaced, for he thought it would be a distraction from the game against Texas Tech. ESPN planned to beam Sanders and his teammates back to the United States by broadcast, but Sanders was reluctant, to say the least:

"It's just not that big a deal for me," he told *Sports Illustrated.* "And it's not really fair to so many other people. People take sports way too seriously. To some of them, sports is a god, which is wrong."

Many, if not most, college football players would never say such a thing. Those few who might choose to do so, to run against the current, would likely be disbelieved. But Barry Sanders was different, the genuine article. While he loved the sport, he saw it as secondary to being a good person, especially in the eyes of his formidable parents.

Then came the announcement. Not only had Sanders won the Heisman Trophy, he had won it by one of the most convincing margins of recent times. He received 1,878 points overall—and 559 first-place votes—to 912 points overall for University of Southern California quarterback Rodney Peete and 582 for UCLA quarterback Troy Aikman.

Sanders was not on hand to receive the award, so his parents and his older brother Byron accepted it for him. The Heisman Trophy was brought to his hometown, where, for a time, it graced the wall in a neighborhood restaurant.

Finally he permitted himself some celebration. Sanders admitted that the award meant a great deal to him, but he made certain to thank and congratulate his teammates, especially the linemen who allowed him to rack up such amazing statistics. There was just one last curtain call to his outstanding year: the Holiday Bowl.

THE BIG GAME

Neither the Wyoming Cowboys nor the OSU players of the same name could be cavalier about a bowl appearance. Invitations went more often to bigger names like Michigan, Ohio State, Notre Dame, and the like. OSU had won the Sun Bowl in 1987, but that had been its first bowl appearance in some time. Wyoming had played in the Holiday Bowl one year before but had lost a painfully close game to Iowa, 20-19.

The Holiday Bowl was not as venerable as some of the others, like the Rose and Cotton bowls; its first game was in 1978. Up to 1988, Brigham Young University had "ruled" the Holiday Bowl, with a total of four wins, but Brigham Young's chance to win again had virtually ended on the first day of the 1988 season, with its disappointing loss to Wyoming.

December 30, 1988, dawned sunny but not mild. Southern California often has the best weather in the nation, but this time around the players from far off would be welcomed by 40-degree temperatures (4.4°C). The weather was nothing

In 1988, the Heisman Trophy, presented to the most outstanding college football player, went to Barry Sanders. On the day the Heisman winner was announced, Sanders was playing in a game against Texas Tech in Japan. Here, he showed off the trophy during a press conference held four days later in New York City.

unusual for men from Oklahoma and Wyoming, but they were a bit surprised to find it in the land of the Beach Boys. Kickoff came in the late afternoon, at Jack Murphy Stadium.

The game started as a sparring match, with each team seeking to find the other's weakness. Sanders broke the game open just five minutes in, with an astonishing 33-yard run for the first score. Commentators on the air simply said, "Matched by none, he holds all the records." Both Cowboy teams scored in the first quarter, making it 7-7, but the OSU Cowboys turned it on in the second quarter, gaining 10 unanswered points: By then, Sanders had two touchdowns. His second came on a two-yard leap over the defenders into the **end zone** (the leap looked eerily like an earlier one in the season that was posted in *Sports Illustrated*'s photos of the year). Quarterback Mike Gundy was also throwing superbly; he ended the day by going 20 for 24 attempts, with a total of 315 yards and two touchdowns. On just about any other day, and with just about any other team, Gundy would have been the Most Valuable Player (MVP) and the person most remembered, but this was Barry Sanders's day, from beginning to end.

Sanders scored after an unbelievable 67-yard run that culminated in a third-quarter touchdown. His Wyoming opponents seemed unable to find their feet as Sanders cruised past them, slipped beyond them, and made it to the goal line. By the end of the third quarter, he had 222 yards **rushing** and five touchdowns; there is little doubt he could have scored another touchdown or two, but the OSU coaches took him out of the game. OSU scored 28 points in that magic third quarter and added 17 unanswered ones in the fourth quarter to make it 62-14, one of the most impressive routs seen in college football that year.

Sports Illustrated came out with its final standings for the year on January 9, 1989. Notre Dame, which had beaten West Virginia in the Fiesta Bowl, was No. 1, an unprecedented eleventh time for the Catholic school. USC, with Rodney Peete as its quarterback, came in seventh, and Oklahoma, OSU's perennial foe, came in at No. 11. But the biggest news, at least to Sanders and his teammates, was that the orange and black of OSU had come in twelfth overall, the school's best showing in many years. And the Wyoming Cowboys? Sadly, the team that had won 10 games in a row was upended by its one regular-season loss and then its defeat in the Holiday Bowl: Wyoming just missed making the Top 20 for the year.

Most keen college football fans believed that Sanders was one of the greatest talents ever seen. What did he have that was so different? First, he had incredible foot speed, an ability to blow past opponents on his way down the field. But to get to the point where he could use that speed, Sanders had to have terrific reflexes and the ability to conceal his own intentions: These he possessed without question. Finally, though, he had a quality that was not so much unique as special: He had the upbringing of his stern but strong parents and 10 siblings to guide his conduct. People often commented that Johnny Unitas, the legendary quarterback for the Baltimore Colts, was so tough because he had had to eat potato soup throughout his youth; the same could be said of Barry Sanders, although he also had a terrible sweet tooth. All those Snickers and Dove bars had not slowed him down, though, and he was rightly considered the outstanding college player of 1988.

Dreams of
Greatness

Well, what if I want 2,500 [yards]?

—Barry Sanders

Barry Sanders entered life at an important time in American history. The Census Bureau determined that the 200 millionth American had been born sometime in 1967, and Barry came into the world at a time when the "generation gap" between middle-aged Americans and their children was at its height. Of course none of this registered on the baby boy from Wichita, Kansas; he only knew that he came to a large and still-growing family.

Barry was born in Wichita on July 16, 1968. His father, William Sanders, was a carpenter and roofer, and his mother, Shirley Sanders, was a homemaker. She had to be a good one because the Sanders family grew to a total of 11 children: Barry was the seventh.

1968 was a year of great tumult in the United States. This was the year of political infighting—at the Democratic National Convention—and of actual fighting in the streets of cities like Chicago. The United States was torn in two by conflicts over the Vietnam War, which had begun a few years earlier. None of this national conflict was felt by young Barry. The challenges he faced were more specific to those of his race and economic status.

THE SANDERS FAMILY

Most children experience their lives as revolving around their mother, and Barry was no exception, but his father was a formidable presence in his life. William Sanders was tall, lean, and almost lanky in a very strongly built manner. His physical presence was mirrored by a powerful personality; Barry later recalled that he and his 10 siblings had no alternative except to say, "Yes Daddy." William Sanders was, quite simply, the boss.

Shirley Sanders was quite different from her stern, demanding husband. She shared his work ethic and values, but she was gentle with the children—at least most of the time. While William concentrated on hard, gritty work and making a living—people who have "roofed" know how hot it can be on top of a building in summertime—she focused on creating an atmosphere of love and compassion in the home. She was a woman who truly feared God, and she imparted this belief to all her 11 children.

Growing up with 10 siblings is a major feat, as anyone born to a large family knows. What is amazing is that 11 siblings all come from the same genetic joining of two people—mother and father—and they are often raised in ways that seem identical, but the children turn out different, anyway. In large families, there is usually an aggressive child, usually a passive one, often one or two who shine at sports, and sometimes two or three who do best in academics. Sometimes others—middle children, especially—seem to slip through the cracks, taking much longer to form their identities. But wherever one is in the birth order, there is no doubt that having a group of siblings has its impact on everyone in the family.

Barry appears to have been a "quiet" one in the large Sanders family. Even photographs from much later in life display a sober, unsmiling Barry when surrounded by his many siblings. This does not mean that he was unhappy (far from it) but that he took on the role of the strong, silent one at an early age and found it difficult to change the habit. He and his two brothers were under special pressure, from their demanding father, to sit up straight, pay attention, and follow the rules.

THE NEIGHBORHOOD

Neighborhood is less a feature of American life today than it was in the years of Barry's childhood in Wichita. There are many reasons for this, including television, computers, and all sorts of things—like automobiles—that take one *away* or out of the neighborhood. But Barry grew up at a time when the American neighborhood was still strong, when the opinions of elders living across the street mattered, and when a troop of children might well walk two miles to a store for a Pepsi-Cola and a candy bar—both of which were considered major treats.

Barry grew up on Volutsia Avenue, a street that he later claimed had produced three significant athletes and a number of outstanding people who contributed to the town, the community, and the state as a whole. Though he was born at a time when segregation was still a big part of American life, Barry did not grow up with a feeling that blacks were inferior or that they were limited in the ways in which they could contribute to society. There were too many examples to the

Barry Sanders and several of his family members got together for a photograph in the 1990s. Barry, who grew up in Wichita, Kansas, was the seventh of 11 children in the Sanders family. His father, William, was a carpenter and roofer, and his mother, Shirley, was a homemaker.

contrary, including hard-working, successful physical laborers like his father. Besides, there was the church.

Church was a major aspect of life for the entire Sanders family. It was only a short walk to the Paradise Baptist Church, and the entire family went most of the time. There were choral practices, too, and special church events at which Mrs. Sanders was often a leading presence. The result was that Barry grew up with a feeling of being watched from all sorts of (loving) directions; he had strong parents, to be sure, but there were also watchful neighbors and co-parishioners. Americans today are divided on the importance of neighborhood and community. Many lament the passing of days when children grew up as Barry did, but others point to the constraints placed upon young people by so many watchful eyes.

SPORTS

Athletic participation was a natural for most of the Sanders children. Their father set a tough example with his rugged physique and strong willpower, but there was also a "love" aspect to sports: Nearly all the Sanders children loved childhood games, which, in the case of the boys especially, turned into a love of competition.

Barry was excited about sports from the very beginning. He played Biddy Basketball, Biddy Football, and the like. But almost from the start of his participation in athletic endeavors, Barry heard the three words that would dog the first half of his life:

He's too small.

These words followed Barry from first grade to almost his senior year in high school. When children chose teams for baseball, they thought he was too small. When he joined the football team in junior high school, the coaches thought he was a midget; perhaps they compared him to his older, bigger brother Byron. Wherever he went, Barry heard that he was too small. But he never let it stop him. This is what he said about the influence of sports in his autobiography, co-written with his childhood friend Mark E. McCormick:

> It would be difficult to underestimate the importance of sports in my childhood. Daddy, a lifelong fan of the Kansas Jayhawk basketball team and Oklahoma Sooner football team, always seemed to have the chatter of a game on the television or on the radio. And in the barbershop, we'd listen to the heated arguments among old men about the failings and fortunes of local and regional teams.

Whether it was table tennis, baseball, basketball, or football, Barry tried out for sports. He seemed to be constantly thinking about sports, even when not playing. Some people said that he had a permanent smile on his face in those junior high and high school years. But there were frustrations.

William Sanders did not become an easier father over the years; in fact he seems to have become more demanding. By his middle teenage years, Barry was helping his father with carpentry and roofing as well as attending high school and playing as many sports as possible. Then, too, the large Sanders family had to scrimp and save to get by. Mrs. Sanders was an accomplished pro at this, and the children seldom went without anything truly important, but there were lots of little extras that went by the wayside.

Barry's "legend" began to develop with his small, close circle of friends during his high school years. He was known for having the largest appetite in almost any group: It was said that he could eat a loaf of bread in one sitting. He had a reputation for a certain close-minded focus that included playing electric football for hours at a time. But he was also developing a fierce work ethic; sometimes in the summer, he would attend football practice in the morning, "roof" with his father in the 100-degree (38°C) afternoon heat, and then show up at evening football practice.

Things would have been even tougher except for Barry's brothers.

Growing up with 10 siblings was difficult enough, but having eight of them be sisters was even harder. When he looked for male role models, Barry saw his demanding, somewhat frightening father, and his two brothers, Boyd and Byron.

Boyd was considerably older than the other two. Early in life he struggled, both with their father's notorious discipline and with the temptations afforded by street life. By the time Barry was in high school, though, Boyd had matured and was on his way to becoming a minister.

Just one year older than Barry, Byron was the leader of the Sanders boys through most of their childhood. Bigger and stronger than Barry, Byron had become a hero to his younger brother, who tagged along as often as he could, both to watch Byron play games and to hang out with his friends. Never competitive among themselves, the two teenagers watched each other blossom on the football field in high school. Both were running backs, but Byron seemed to have the bigger future ahead; in his senior year he was recruited by Northwestern. And Barry? He would be lucky to make it to Wichita State.

1980s FOOTBALL

Any great player—Barry Sanders included—grows up watching or, in previous days, listening, to the games of his youth. What was football like in the late 1970s and early 1980s, when Barry was a youngster?

The Pittsburgh Steelers were dominant in the late 1970s, with quarterback Terry Bradshaw possessing one of the best arms ever seen, but the running game was better displayed by the Dallas Cowboys. Known as "America's Team," the Cowboys had a terrific quarterback in Roger Staubach and an equally great running back in Tony Dorsett. Earl Campbell, playing for the Houston Oilers, was also making a name for himself, as was Billy Sims of the Detroit Lions. Barry doubtless admired all these great backs, but the biggest attention was paid to two who had become memories: O.J. Simpson of the Buffalo Bills and Jim Brown of the Cleveland Browns.

Barry was too young to remember Jim Brown, who ended his football career in the summer of 1966, but Barry's father absolutely idolized Brown, calling him a man among boys

THE COLLEGE GAME

Barry applied to plenty of schools, but only two offered him athletic scholarships: Wichita State and Oklahoma State University (OSU). Wichita State seemed too close—it was less than a mile away. Barry greatly desired to play for the University of Oklahoma, the Sooners whom he had watched since childhood, but Oklahoma head coach Barry Switzer felt that he could not afford an athletic scholarship for so small a player—Barry Sanders was 5-foot-8 (173 centimeters). With no other offers coming in, Barry decided on the OSU Cowboys.

on the football field. As for O.J. Simpson, his career was over by the time Barry entered high school, but millions of young boys around the nation aspired to be the next "Juice," slashing their way through a set of defensive linemen. Nor did it hurt that O.J. had become the highest-paid black football player.

As much as Barry loved the game, he, and millions of other fans, had reason for discontent in the early and mid-1980s. There was a players' strike in the autumn of 1982, leading to a shortened season. There was a start-up rival league, the United States Football League, which took the National Football League (NFL) to court. And by the late 1980s there was a heightened awareness of the presence of steroids—performance-enhancing drugs—in the sport.

Happily Barry did not let the diminished state of the game deter him from seeking the fulfillment of his life dream. When he reached the pros, Barry determined that he would never be the object of an investigation or a scandal.

Showing up at OSU in Stillwater in the late summer of 1986, Barry found that he had competition. Thurman Thomas (who later played for the Buffalo Bills) was two years older and a fair bit wiser. He was the starting running back for the Cowboys that year and the following season as well.

Though he spent plenty of time on the bench and though he continued to hear the occasional whisper of "midget," Barry settled in for what could be a long haul. He gained 325 yards on 74 carries in 1986, not bad considering he was a second-string running back. That summer he stayed at OSU, bagged groceries for a time, and enjoyed the relative freedom from Wichita. Then came the electrifying moment of September 9, 1987.

On the first play of the first game of his sophomore season, Barry, as the kick returner, took the opening kickoff and ran it 100 yards for a touchdown. To say this was extraordinary does not fully embrace its importance; here he was, a second-string player, doing what first-rate ones usually did not accomplish. That dramatic opening run set Barry on fire and made for a much better season than his freshman year (he ran for 622 yards on 111 carries). He still labored, though, in the shadow of Thomas, who had a truly outstanding year (1,613 yards on 251 carries).

Still, even in the background, Barry garnered notice. University of Oklahoma head coach Barry Switzer, who had built a terrific program over the years, surprised many of his defensive players by telling them, after he watched a series of game tapes, that they had better hope that Thomas was not injured. Why, they wondered? Because OSU had a backup runner in Barry who would be much worse—"you won't even touch this guy," Switzer said.

After the 1987 season, Thomas left for the Buffalo Bills, and Barry became OSU's starting running back. Against Miami, he opened the season by taking another kickoff and running it 100 yards for a touchdown, becoming the first player in college

After receiving two scholarship offers, Barry Sanders decided to attend Oklahoma State University. Here, he slid past Colorado defender Cole Hayes during a game in 1988, his junior year. During that season, Sanders broke 25 NCAA records, including the single-season marks for rushing yards and touchdowns.

football ever to begin two seasons in a row with touchdown returns. That was just the beginning.

Barry had one of the most remarkable seasons of any college player in the history of the sport. By season's end, he had racked up more yards (2,628) and touchdowns (39), and had a higher yards-per-**carry** (7.6) average than anyone else in memory. He had rushed for an average of more than 200 yards per game. He won the Heisman Trophy by a landslide and was considered, potentially, the No. 1 pick in the NFL **Draft** of 1989.

He was, however, only a junior. According to NFL and college rules at the time, Barry would have to play his fourth, senior, season to become eligible for the NFL Draft. Then fate intervened.

The NCAA had been investigating Oklahoma State Unviersity for some time, and the results were released in the winter of 1989. Because of the school's violation of certain recruiting rules, OSU games would not be shown on television during the 1989 season and the university would not be eligible for any college bowls. It was a heartbreaker for the OSU team but unexpected luck for Barry. Given that Barry's potential was obvious, the NFL commissioner, Pete Rozelle, decided to allow him to participate in the 1989 NFL Draft.

He hesitated.

College life had been good to Barry; he wasn't sure he wanted to leave. But, not for the first time in life, he was influenced by his father.

William Sanders was furious that his son was even thinking about staying at OSU. College football was good, to be sure, but it could not hold a candle to the money Barry could make as a promising first-year NFL player. Barry later described, in his autobiography, what the scene was like:

> I listened to Daddy for hours, literally hours, scream and curse at me for even considering a return for my senior year in Stillwater. I'd never seen him so emotional.

Shirley Sanders thought it should be Barry's decision. She had prevailed over her husband many times over the years, persuading him to take a softer tone with the children, but on this occasion he was adamant. Barry put it succinctly:

"I folded."

He entered the NFL Draft.

Shown in a 1989 photo, Detroit Lions head coach Wayne Fontes took Barry Sanders on a tour of the Lions' locker room at the Pontiac Silverdome. The Lions selected Sanders with the third overall pick in the 1989 NFL Draft.

THE 1989 DRAFT

Many observers of the game, including sports historian Michael MacCambridge, have noted that the 1989 NFL Draft marked a significant departure. Barry was one of the most promising players, but there were others, including the enormously muscular and heavily tattooed Tony Mandarich, an offensive **tackle**. There was also the incomparable **cornerback** Deion Sanders, who had made such a splash during his years at Florida State. Deion and Barry were a study in contrasts, with the former making an extravaganza out of every play and the latter playing down all his accomplishments. Coaches and fans may have preferred Barry to Deion, but Deion was more in step with the times: "Prime Time," as Deion called it, had arrived.

The Detroit Lions had their eye on Barry. The Lions had had a terrible 1988 season, going 4–12, but their record allowed them one of the first choices in the NFL Draft. Head coach Wayne Fontes and assistant head coach Dave Levy went to Oklahoma State to see what Barry Sanders was like. Levy had a conversation with Barry but found the Oklahoma State player not very talkative. Suddenly Barry said, "I'll lift for you." He went to the weight bench and lifted 225 pounds (102 kilograms) 21 times. He asked the coach, Was that good? Yes, that was just fine, was the answer.

Fontes, who had taken over as the Lions' coach partway through the 1988 season, was much more relaxed in his personal style than many NFL coaches. Barry, however, challenged Fontes and Levy, saying that he was a wingback and wondering how he would fit in with Detroit's new **"run and shoot" offense**. Levy responded gently, telling Barry that he believed that the Lions' new offense would allow the sensational running back to get as many as 1,500 rushing yards in a season, to which Barry replied, "Well what if I want 2,500?" Both coaches allowed that that would be fine with them.

The announcement was made on April 24, 1989. With major media from around the nation watching, Fontes declared that Barry would be a Lion. Barry then stepped to the microphone where, in his laconic style, he said he felt really good about the decision and that he hoped to be one of a number of players who would "restore the roar" to the Silverdome.

He was given the choice of taking No. 20, which had previously belonged to Billy Sims, Detroit's great running back from 1980 to 1984. And so Barry Sanders, No. 21 for Oklahoma State, became No. 20 for the Detroit Lions.

Rookie Rusher

Let Christian [Okoye] have it.

—Barry Sanders

Anyone who has ever played in the NFL will say, when asked, that the **rookie** year is the hardest. Many players never make it out of their rookie year; Barry Sanders's very talented older brother Byron was one. After a fine career as a running back at Northwestern University, Byron was drafted by the Chicago Bears but was cut from the team after just two months.

THE SILVERDOME
The Detroit Lions of 1989 played in the Pontiac Silverdome, about 30 miles (48 kilometers) from downtown Detroit.

Completed in 1975 and opened for the Lions' season of that year, the Silverdome was a showcase for the "indoor" game that sprouted up in that decade and for the AstroTurf that became a fixture on many playing fields. When he was first chosen by the Lions, Sanders expressed his appreciation by saying that he hoped to be among those who would "restore the roar" to the dome.

The Lions had been a powerhouse in the late 1940s and throughout the 1950s. Originally known as the Portsmouth (Ohio) Spartans, they had come northwest to Detroit in the 1930s and had turned out many sensational players, including the remarkable quarterback Bobby Layne. The 1960s and 1970s, though, had not been kind to the Lions, who were passed by teams such as the Green Bay Packers (a perennial opponent) and the Chicago Bears, who had practically ruled the game in the mid-1980s. Detroit's only real bright spot of the past decade had been the running of Billy Sims.

Sanders held out for the best contract he could obtain. The matter was settled just days before the regular season began, meaning that Sanders missed almost all of summer camp and preseason play. He finally settled for a contract that gave him $9.5 million over five years. There was plenty of criticism to go around, with pundits claiming that the young rookie cared only about the cash, but most of the criticism was silenced when the public learned that Sanders handed 10 percent of his **signing bonus**, $250,000, to his Baptist church back home in Wichita. All the talk and negotiating did take its toll, however, and Sanders reported to the Lions only three days before the season opener against the Phoenix Cardinals.

Detroit had gone 4–12 the previous year and, with the exception of Sanders's appearance, there was no reason to think 1989 would be that different. For the first half of the season opener, Sanders was on the sidelines; coach Wayne Fontes was waiting for the right moment to use his new star. When asked

Barry Sanders is shown during a press conference in 1989 after signing his first NFL contract. Sanders missed much of training camp as negotiations over the contract dragged out. Some critics said he only cared about the money, but many people changed their minds after hearing that he donated $250,000—10 percent of his signing bonus—to his church in Wichita, Kansas.

in the middle of the third quarter, Sanders answered in a nonchalant way that yes, he was ready to go.

He came on to a very loud burst of applause; Lions fans knew of his record at Oklahoma State and hoped he would give them a special performance. Later Sanders admitted that, just like any other NFL rookie, he was nervous at that moment; he had not been "hit" by defensive linemen since the Holiday Bowl eight months ago, and he had never been hit by NFL linemen. On his very first down as a professional NFL player, Sanders received a handoff from quarterback Bob Gagliano. (Rodney Peete, with whom Barry had competed for the 1988 Heisman Trophy, had been drafted in the sixth round by the Lions. He was set to be their starting quarterback but was out with an injury received in an exhibition game.)

Sanders did a slant right, then a slant left, and suddenly he burst through the **line of scrimmage**. Running, chugging, and churning—one often runs out of words when describing his play—Sanders rushed for 19 yards and got a **first down** on his very first NFL play. Minutes later, he ran the ball in for six points. Showing the style that would make him famous, Sanders did not spike the ball or do any shenanigans; he simply tossed the ball to the official on the left-hand side and jogged back to his teammates.

If the crowd was excited before, it now went wild. Sanders seemed to demonstrate his potential from this very moment forward. But like every other NFL rookie, he would take his lumps of coal along with the dashes of sugar. He and the Lions did not win that day: They lost to the Cardinals, 16-13, on a field goal with just seconds left in the game.

Sanders's first away game came the following week, on September 17. Quarterback Rodney Peete remained out with an injury, so Gagliano, the backup, came in to perform magnificently, passing for 344 yards. **Wide receiver** Richard Johnson caught nine passes for 172 yards that day, but these incredible efforts were insufficient: The New York Giants won 24-14.

Sanders was relatively "quiet" in the loss to the Giants, but he came on with a roar against the Chicago Bears on September 24. At the Silverdome, he rushed for 126 yards as he and the Lions went down to defeat 47-27. He came away from the game with some bruised ribs and a **hip pointer** that bothered him for the rest of the season. Sanders later described the AstroTurf as "basically pavement covered by a thin green rug." The fourth regular-season game was at Pittsburgh, where the Lions were thumped 23-3. The season was off to a very bad beginning, but Sanders was already making headlines. The attention only increased after Game 5, in which the Minnesota Vikings head coach asked officials to investigate if Sanders had rubbed silicone or some other substance on his legs—that was how difficult it was to get a grip on him. The officials found nothing untoward as Sanders rushed for 99 yards. The Vikings prevailed 24-17, however, meaning that Detroit was 0–5.

Redemption finally arrived on Sunday, October 15, when the Lions edged Tampa Bay 17-16 in the narrowest of victories. Rodney Peete, now in at quarterback, ran in the winning score with 23 seconds left on the clock, and Detroit had its first win of the season. Sanders, though, sat out the game with an injury. One week later, the Lions went to Minnesota to play the Vikings, a team that was traditionally one of the hardest for them to beat. There had been a terrible drought from 1969 to 1974, in which the Lions never defeated the Vikings. (Because the two teams are in the same division, they play each other twice every season.) Again, the Lions did not have an answer for the Vikings, as Minnesota won 20-7.

Detroit then played another of its perennial rivals. The Green Bay Packers had been a terrific powerhouse in the 1960s, had faded a bit in the 1970s, and were now coming on strong. Both the Packers and the Lions were truly "physical" teams, the type that liked to butt heads, but the Packers usually had more weight on their **offensive line**. This time it was a terrific slugfest, with the outcome in doubt all afternoon long. Sanders had his best NFL performance to date, rushing for 184 yards, but the Lions fell 23-20.

Detroit was 1–7. Could the season get any worse?

It did. On Sunday, November 5, the Lions traveled to Houston and went down to defeat against the Oilers, 35-31. At this point Detroit was 1–8, with the worst record in the league. The team was becoming the laughing stock of the NFL.

Coach Wayne Fontes saw it differently. No one felt the pain of the season more than he did, but Fontes saw potential. His new quarterback, Peete, was slowly adjusting to the "Silver Stretch" run-and-shoot offense patented at Detroit. His star running back, Sanders, was getting better with each game. As bad as the scoreboard looked, Fontes believed the team would improve. And finally it did, on Sunday, November 12, when the Lions beat the Green Bay Packers at the Silverdome 31-22. Even so, one more humiliaton waited in the wings.

The Cincinnati Bengals came to town on Sunday, November 19. Sanders had a fine performance, rushing for 114 yards, but the Bengals thrashed the daylights out of the Lions, 42-7. Detroit was now 2–9 for the year.

Questioned about the defeat, Fontes admitted that it had been a humiliating experience. When he went to the locker room to address his players, he chose not to rant and rave, speaking instead about the character of the team and how it would emerge in the games to come. He told his men to "hold their heads high" and to expect future victories.

FINALLY WINNING

That loss was the last one Sanders had to stomach in 1989. The Lions went on a tear following their defeat by the Bengals. Detroit beat Cleveland 13-10 in the Lions' annual Thanksgiving game, a day that saw Sanders rush for 145 yards (he had 189 total yards that day). On Sunday, December 3, the Lions beat the New Orleans Saints, another team that had struggled throughout the 1970s and 1980s. This was the first pair of back-to-back victories the Lions had enjoyed in three years.

Barry Sanders made a cut down the field during a game on December 10, 1989, against the Chicago Bears. The Lions had gotten off to an abysmal 2–9 start during Sanders's rookie year. Detroit was able to turn its season around, and in this game, the Lions defeated the Bears 27-17.

Sanders had 120 yards rushing on Sunday, December 10, as the Lions defeated the Chicago Bears, 27-17, at Soldier Field. The Bears had fallen hard since their salad days of 1985. The best for the Lions was yet to come.

On Sunday, December 17, the Lions handily defeated Tampa Bay in a home game that saw Sanders rush for 104 yards. In so doing, he beat the Lions' previous rookie rushing record, held by Billy Sims. Play was stopped for 15 minutes, and Sims jogged onto the field to hug Sanders (it looked like a bear crushing its cub) and hold his hand up to an appreciative audience.

There was one more game to go, and on December 24, Sanders rushed for 158 yards and three touchdowns as the Lions edged the Atlanta Falcons, 31-24. That win made it five

THE ROARING TWENTIES

Billy Sims and Barry Sanders shared a number of things in common. Both played for Oklahoma teams (Sims with the University of Oklahoma), both were Heisman Trophy winners, and both became running backs for the Detroit Lions. The difference, of course, was nine years: Sims came in 1980 and Sanders in 1989. They even shared the same team number, 20.

Sims had been an outstanding member of the Lions from 1980 to 1984, but fans most remembered his remarkable rookie season in which he rushed for 1,303 yards, with a yards-per-carry average of 4.2 and 13 touchdowns. His rushing yardage set a Lions record for a rookie. It seemed incredible that Sanders—or anyone else—would break Sims's record, but as the commentators frequently remind us, records are meant to be broken.

As the 1989 season progressed, it became clear that Sanders had a chance to surpass Sims's record, provided he remained healthy. Sanders gained ground through October and November, and by December 17, when the Lions faced Tampa Bay, he was close enough to see the hash marks. Sanders had a spectacular day, rushing for 104 yards, and play was stopped for 15 minutes at the moment in which he broke Sims's rookie rushing record (Sanders went on to gain 1,470 yards, to average 5.3 yards per carry, and to score 14 touchdowns in that rookie year). Sims came on the field to hug Sanders: This was one moment that the two champion-style runners wanted to share.

Will Sanders's rookie-season rushing record for the Lions ever be broken? Very likely, and, knowing Sanders, he will act with the same class that Sims did in 1989.

Former Detroit Lions running back Billy Sims hugged Barry Sanders during a game on December 17, 1989, after Sanders broke Sims's rookie rushing record of 1,303 yards. Sanders would go on to rush for 1,470 yards during his debut season, and he was named the NFL Rookie of the Year.

in a row, a feat Detroit had not accomplished since the 1970 season, played when Barry was just two years old.

Late in the game, Fontes discovered that his star rookie player was 11 yards shy of winning the NFL rushing title (Christian Okoye of the Kansas City Chiefs had 10 yards on him). With minutes left to play, Fontes felt it was almost a certainty that Sanders would get his 11 yards and win a coveted prize. Sanders, though, only shrugged and said the game was as good as won. "Let Christian have it," he said.

Moments like this do not come very often. Most NFL players—rookies or seasoned veterans—strive for everything they can get, and if a record appears within their grasp, they make a 100 percent effort. Either Sanders genuinely did not care that much about the statistic (and many of his later comments suggest this) or he felt it was unseemly to chase records. In either case, he won the appreciation of thousands of fans who witnessed the appearance of a terrific running back who was not enthralled to his own ego.

Sanders was never big on talking about himself or his accomplishments, but toward the end of that rookie year he allowed himself to wax a little: "I try to perfect the art of making people miss. . . . If you have that and speed, what more do you need?" When asked about the rushing title and other numbers, Sanders waved off the question, "Stats and stuff, I don't get caught up in it. . . . I like to think we're going to build a winning tradition here."

Sanders's rookie year was nothing to be sad about. He rushed for 1,470 yards on 280 attempts, with an average per-rush gain of 5.3 yards. He scored 14 touchdowns. He was selected as an All-Pro running back and played in the **Pro Bowl** in Honolulu. Most gratifying of all, he was selected as the NFL Rookie of the Year.

Solid Gold

I can't be sad about the 27 years of her life.

—Barry Sanders

The Detroit Lions had recovered from a terrible beginning in 1989 to finish at 7–9. That record was nothing to brag about, but the team showed real potential for the future.

A NEW YEAR

Most Americans mark January 1 as the start of their calendars, but NFL players generally think of the first Sunday of the football season as the key date. On September 9, 1990, the Detroit Lions met one of their perennial foes, the Tampa Bay Buccaneers.

It was not just that the two teams met often and that they had demanding games. There was something special to this rivalry between one of the NFL's oldest teams (the Lions), which had been on a losing streak for some time, and one of its newest (the Buccaneers), which was picking up momentum. Detroit prided itself on the Silver Stretch offense, while Tampa delighted in all sorts of defensive specialties.

Tampa beat Detroit, 38-21.

It was a dismal beginning to the season, but the Lions came back to beat the Atlanta Falcons on September 16, 21-14. Barry Sanders had not yet had a breakout game; he was gaining steady yardage but had not exploded with the kind of speed for which he was becoming famous.

There followed another game against Tampa Bay, and Detroit lost this one as well, by 23-20. A loss to Green Bay on September 30 put the Lions at 1–3 for the season, dampening spirits all around. It seemed that the Lions had nowhere to go. If they traveled south for a game with Tampa Bay, they were edged; and if they played in the northern climes to which they were accustomed, they got beat.

Next up was Minnesota, the toughest team historically for the Lions to beat.

On this day in 1990, the Lions fought like wildcats, putting up an excellent contest, and this time they won, 27-24.

Then came a matchup with Kansas City. The Chiefs were a tough opponent for many teams, but the Lions had roughly a .500 record against them, so it was believed the game could go either way. Sanders starred in the contest, rushing for 90 yards, catching five passes for 135 yards, and scoring two touchdowns. Sanders's production, though, was not enough, as Kansas City prevailed, 43-24. At this point, the Lions were 2–4.

Everyone had counted the Lions out for the season, but coach Wayne Fontes felt that his team's pride was on the line. The Lions could not sit back and take this punishment; they had to deal out some of their own. So it was with great satisfaction that Detroit recorded its third win of 1990, beating the New Orleans Saints 27-10. One week later, the Lions played the

Washington Redskins. Sanders rushed for 104 yards that day, but the Redskins took the game, 41-38.

To say that the 1990 Lions were a "tough luck" team is an understatement. Listen to the comments of frustrated fan Barry Schumer, who wrote *I Don't Believe It: Memories of a Detroit Lions Fan*:

> September 9, 1990, a new season, a new decade, a new result? Nope, Tampa wins 38-21; the Lions have 6 turnovers and are sacked 6 times. . . . October 28, 1990, a great birthday present for me—Lions beat the Saints 27-10 forcing 8 turnovers. Shouldn't you score more than 27 when you get 8 turnovers? November 4, 1990, the Redskins win 41-38 in overtime—Detroit led 35-14 in the third.

The Lions seemed to find every possible way to lose in the first half of 1990. The season finally got better on November 11, when Detroit beat the Minnesota Vikings 17-7; a win, any win, against the Vikings was a special moment. But Detroit was thrashed by the New York Giants, 20-0, the next Sunday, bringing up one of Detroit's most beloved traditions, the annual Thanksgiving Day game. This year, it was a matchup between Detroit and the Denver Broncos.

Detroit beat John Elway and the Denver Broncos, 40-27. Sanders rushed for 147 yards that day, winning appreciation from both his Detroit fans and a nationwide audience. There followed a loss to the Chicago Bears, 23-17, and a painful loss to the Los Angeles Raiders on *Monday Night Football*, 38-31 (Sanders rushed for 176 yards that night—his best game of the season). At least the Lions were keeping these games close. They closed out the difficult season in style, beating the Chicago Bears, 38-21 (a day in which Rodney Peete passed for 316 yards) and Green Bay by 24-17 (a day that saw Sanders rush for 133 yards), before falling to the Seattle Seahawks, 30-10. All told, the 1990

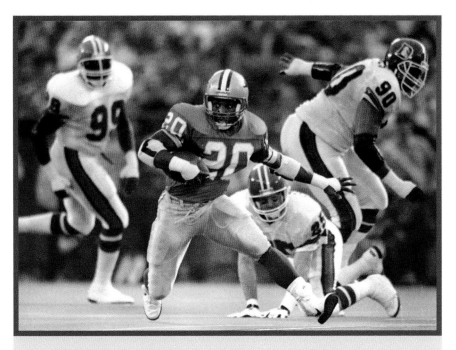

Barry Sanders left a trail of Denver Broncos defenders behind him during a run in the Lions' annual Thanksgiving Day game in 1990. Sanders rushed for 147 yards in the game, which Detroit won 40-27. The Thanksgiving Day game has been a Lions tradition since 1934, the first year the team played in the Motor City.

Detroit Lions had a 6–10 record, finishing in a four-way tie for second place in the NFC Central Division with Minnesota, Green Bay, and Tampa Bay. (Chicago won the division with an 11–5 record.)

BIGGER CHALLENGES

Barry Sanders may have been frustrated by his team's performance in 1990, but he had bigger issues with which to cope. During the winter of 1991, his older sister Nancy came to live with him in Michigan. The two had always been close, and she needed help. Nancy was suffering from scleroderma, a chronic disease characterized by excessive deposits of collagen on the skin or other organs.

THE THANKSGIVING DAY GAME

Norman Rockwell never painted a major football canvas, but if he had, one suspects that Thanksgiving would have been featured.

For most Americans, Thanksgiving is a special day, complete with turkey, gravy, and mashed potatoes, a celebration of American plenty. But ever since the Lions started a tradition of playing football on Thanksgiving afternoons, there has been another side to the American holiday.

It began in 1934, when the Great Depression was in full swing.

The Lions had just moved to Detroit from Ohio, where they had been known as the Portsmouth Spartans. Playing a Thanksgiving Day game was originally a gimmick, designed to increase the ticket proceeds for the owners, but it soon developed into a tradition: Only from 1939 to 1944, the World War II years, was there no Thanksgiving Day game in Detroit.

Television helped, of course, and by the 1950s the Turkey Day game was a classic, drawing fans from around the nation. Detroit had its best Thanksgiving Day games in the 1950s, the era of quarterback Bobby Layne, when they won eight out of 10. Perhaps their proudest moment was on Thanksgiving Day 1962, when they beat Vince Lombardi's Green Bay Packers: That was Green Bay's only loss that year. Lombardi was so upset that he refused to bring his Packers to any more Turkey Day games.

Detroit fared less well in the 1970s and 1980s, but there was always the possibility of an upset. For every tough loss they took, the Lions administered at least one sound defeat, often upending teams with much better records; it seemed that Detroit saved its best play for Turkey Day. As of the end of 2007, the Lions were 33–33–2 in Thanksgiving Day games, and the tradition seemed set to last well into the twenty-first century.

The Sanders family was very tight, but family members expressed their love in an inclusive way. Having 11 children meant that Shirley Sanders had become a mother to many other neighborhood children. There were no favorites in the Sanders homestead; everyone had to share, tighten their belts on occasion, and get along. But when Barry became an NFL star, with more money than anyone in the family could ever have dreamed, he was able to help his parents—buying them a large home in Wichita—and he welcomed Nancy into his home (a three-minute drive from the Silverdome) to administer his own brand of tender, loving care. Years later, in his autobiography *Now You See Him...*, Sanders expressed his feelings for his sister:

> Nancy always seemed to be there when I needed her. When I was about three years old, Mother took Nancy and me on a ride to where my daddy worked to bring him lunch. I was in Nancy's lap. Mother said when she turned a corner, the door of our old station wagon flew open, and Nancy and I were jolted onto the street. Either from fear or from pure instinct, Nancy wrapped me in a bear hug and made sure that when we hit the pavement, I landed on her.

Neither child was hurt in the accident.

Barry was delighted to have Nancy live with him in the spring and summer of 1991, but he was pained to watch her rather swift demise. The disease (about 300,000 Americans suffer from it) has no cure. If the disease remains localized, it tends not to be fatal. Diffuse scleroderma will generally cause more internal-organ damage and is generally more life-threatening.

As Barry entered the 1991 football season, he knew his sister was dying. They did not talk about it very much, and she refused to succumb to self-pity. Instead she enrolled in a master's program in music at Langston University in Oklahoma. One weekend that autumn she drove from Langston to Wichita. She made it to the Sanders home, but an ambulance was quickly called, and she died hours later. Barry expressed his thoughts about Nancy:

> I can't be sad about the 27 years of her life, much of which I got to experience. It was a gift, a blessing, a joy, and a privilege. I was fortunate to be her brother. A newspaper reporter wrote in Nancy's obituary that William Sanders says if you think his son is tough, you should have known his daughter Nancy. How true.

This was not the only close-up view Sanders had of death and disablement that autumn.

THE 1991 SEASON

1990 had been a painful year, full of disappointment on the field, and Sanders and the Lions started 1991 full of desire to win back their spurs (figuratively). His football year began with difficulty, however. Sanders asked the Lions management to restructure his contract (allowing more money and more incentives to be built into the deal), and the resulting salary dispute meant that Sanders barely made it to training camp before the season began. Injured in a preseason game against the Kansas City Chiefs (it was a painful rib injury), he sat out the opening game against the Washington Redskins: Detroit was slaughtered 45-0, its worst loss in more than 20 years.

Sanders was healthy and able to play in the second game of the season, at home against Green Bay, and the Lions gained some confidence with a 23-14 win. One week later, they played Dan Marino and the Miami Dolphins. There were some tense moments as the Dolphins drove deep into Lions territory with less than five minutes left. The Dolphins had a first and goal,

In a game against the Indianapolis Colts on September 22, 1991, Barry Sanders rushed for 179 yards and two touchdowns. Playing against Sanders on the Colts was famed running back Eric Dickerson, but he was held to a career-low 17 rushing yards that day.

but Detroit's much-improved defense (it had been last in the league in 1990) kept them from the end zone, slapping away a pass on fourth and goal. Sanders rushed for 143 yards as the Lions held on to win, 17-13. Then came a matchup against the Indianapolis Colts.

Now with the Colts, Eric Dickerson—who set the single-season rushing record in 1983 with 2,105 yards—was no longer as sensational a running back as he had been, say, four years earlier. He was still good, however, and the game was seen beforehand as something of a contest between him and Sanders. In this game, though, it was no contest: Sanders rushed for a whopping 179 yards and two touchdowns, while the Lions' defense held Dickerson to a career-low 17 rushing yards. With Detroit's 33-24 victory, people started to whisper about the "new" Lions team.

Revenge is sweet, but it is a dish often served cold. The Lions had experienced many turnovers and close losses to Tampa Bay over the years, but they dished it out in handsome style on September 29, thrashing the Buccaneers 31-3. Sanders gained 160 rushing yards, including a sensational 69-yard touchdown run, which lifted the Lions to 4–1, with four wins in a row. Seven days later, in Week 6 of the NFL season, the Lions edged the Minnesota Vikings, 24-20, in a game that saw Sanders scramble for 116 rushing yards. In the best comeback attempt anyone in Detroit could recall, the Lions rallied from a 20-3 deficit in the last seven minutes. Sanders had 69 of his rushing yards in the fourth quarter, and he ran 15 yards for the game-winning touchdown with 36 seconds left. There was no doubt in anyone's mind that No. 20 was the key to Detroit's offense and that, when in doubt, one should "give the ball to Barry." Then came the thunderclap.

The San Francisco 49ers were one of the top NFL teams of the age; quarterback Joe Montana had won four Super Bowls along the way. The 49ers wiped out the Lions on October 20, by the unhealthy score of 35-3. To this point, the Lions had done so well that people were actually beginning to mutter the magic word "playoffs," but their big loss to the 49ers seemed to underscore the weaknesses with which they contended. Could a team with so many defeats and setbacks in its history actually become a playoff contender?

Detroit fans answered any doubts by showing up in record numbers the following Sunday; it was, in fact, the first sell-out at home in the past seven years. The Lions themselves answered the question on October 27 by beating the Dallas Cowboys 34-10. Cowboys quarterback Troy Aikman—who was on his way to becoming one of the best of the decade— passed for 331 yards, but the Lions still held him to 10 points. One week later, Detroit took a dive, falling to the Chicago Bears by 20-10. They still held a 6–3 record, much better than in previous years.

On November 10, Detroit lost a painful one to Tampa Bay, 30-21, even though Sanders rushed for 118 yards. One week later, on November 17, Detroit was leading the Los Angeles Rams in a home game when disaster struck. In Sanders's words:

> We didn't know the seriousness or the nature of his injury at the time. We all just stood there, eyes wide, breathing softly and waiting impatiently for him to get up. It seemed like we stood there for an hour. Before long, players from both teams had joined hands, knelt right there on the field, and prayed. A nervous murmur vibrated through the crowd as emergency medical staff hovered over him.

Mike Utley, who hailed from Seattle, Washington, had been with the Lions for three years, the same amount of time as Sanders. The right **guard** had been having a good, though not a sensational, season, when, in blocking a defender, he snapped some vertebrae in his spine. As Sanders expressed it, none of the Lions knew the extent or the seriousness of his injury, but they feared the worst. As if to encourage his teammates—and

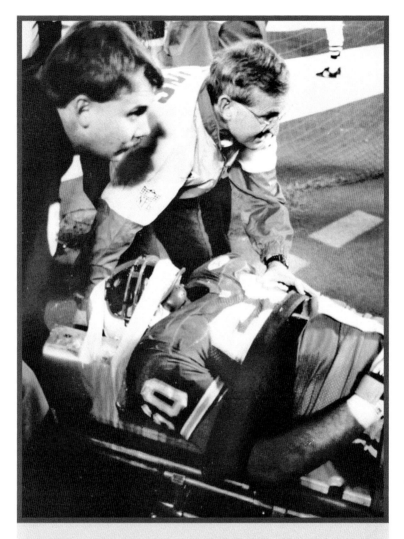

Attendants carried Detroit Lions guard Mike Utley off the field after he sustained a spinal-cord injury in a game against the Los Angeles Rams on November 17, 1991. After seeing their teammate severely injured—Utley would be paralyzed—the Lions vowed to push forward for the season.

to prevent them from worrying about him—Utley gave a "thumbs-up" as he was carried off the field.

The Lions won the game 21-10. In Utley's injury they had found a cause around which to rally.

Thumbs Up

"After the guy hit me, I was still on my feet. That was pretty much it." Right. And the Mona Lisa's a cartoon.
—*from a* Sports Illustrated *article*

No one really knows what life will bring. Most of us have moments when we feel on top of the world, only to see them replaced by times when we are down in the dumps. That unpredictability sometimes motivates us to work, or play, even harder. So it was with the Detroit Lions in the last two months of 1991.

THE WORKHORSE

Seeing Mike Utley carried off the field reinforced Barry Sanders's fear and those of his teammates. Everyone on the field that day knew it could have been he who was carried off on a stretcher. Utley's injury had left him paralyzed. But instead of allowing this fear to cast a pall on the season, Sanders and his teammates vowed to carry on with even more spirit than before. "Thumbs up" became the symbol for the rest of the season, a tangible reminder of the danger in which they lived and the way they expected to overcome the fear that it caused.

Was it only a coincidence that Sanders had the best day—thus far—of his NFL career seven days after Utley's injury? On November 24, he and the Lions stomped the Minnesota Vikings 34-14 in a game that saw Sanders rush for 220 yards and four touchdowns.

Two hundred and twenty! People had to look in all sorts of record books to find an equal to this performance. Many a college back—including Sanders —had done better than this, but few NFL backs had ever exceeded 200 yards. It was around this time that some observers began to compare Barry Sanders with the greatest of them all, Jim Brown.

On November 28, Thanksgiving Day, the Lions hosted the Chicago Bears in what was a tight, nail-biting contest. This time it was the Lions' defense that shone, besting the Bears 16-6. That made it three wins in a row since the loss to the Buccaneers.

On December 8, the Lions defeated the New York Jets 34-20. Sanders had two touchdowns on the day. Quarterback Erik Kramer was sensational, but the Lions had no less than three players sustain season-ending injuries. One week later they beat Green Bay (it was becoming a habit!), 21-17. Detroit fans watching the game saw the "crawl" at the bottom of their television sets declare that this game had sealed a playoff bid for the Lions. And on the final day of the 1991 season, Detroit beat Buffalo (which starred Thurman Thomas as running back) in overtime, by 17-14. Sanders carried the day, with 108 rushing yards.

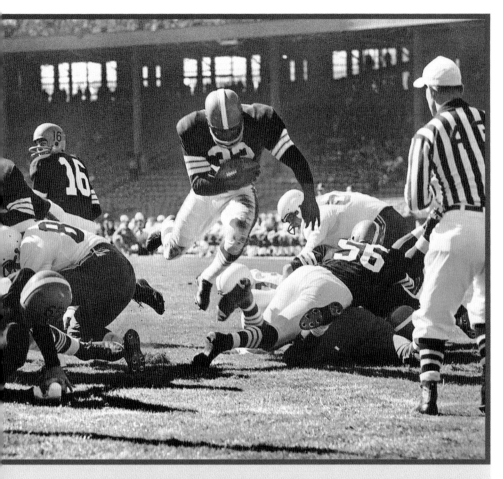

Fullback Jim Brown of the Cleveland Browns tore through a hole for a three-yard touchdown in a 1958 game against the Chicago Cardinals. During Barry Sanders's 1991 season, football insiders began to make comparisons between Sanders and Brown. To Sanders's father, though, Jim Brown would always be the best.

Detroit was crowned the NFC Central Division champ for 1991. The Lions had improved from 6–10 the year before to 12–4, one of the best one-year turnarounds of that decade. Wayne Fontes was named the NFL Coach of the Year, and Sanders finished second in the NFL in rushing yards, with 1,548 yards on 342 carries. (Dallas Cowboy Emmitt Smith was first, with 1,563 yards on 365 carries.)

THE PLAYOFFS

It had been so long since Detroit had made the playoffs that fans had to check their yearbooks. The last time the Lions had played in the postseason was 1982, and the last NFL title they won was back in 1957, when a young, inspiring Bobby Layne was the quarterback. Whether it was the tragic injury to Mike Utley, or the inspired running of Barry Sanders, or an entire, massive effort by the whole team, the Lions had reached the postseason.

Because of their record, the Lions had a bye in the first round of the playoffs. Their first postseason game came against the Dallas Cowboys, who were on the verge of making a great 1990s run. Everyone remembered the days of Tom Landry, Roger Staubach, and Tony Dorsett, but those players and coaches were now gone, replaced by Jimmy Johnson, Troy Aikman, and Emmitt Smith. Dallas had made a terrific effort to rebuild and, given the Cowboys' long tradition of postseason play, most observers gave them the edge against the Lions.

The two teams met on January 5, 1992. Lions quarterback Rodney Peete was still out with an injury, so the challenge fell to the broad shoulders and quick wit of Erik Kramer, who rose to it with a vengeance. Here is how *Sports Illustrated* described his performance:

> Kramer finished with 29 completions in 38 attempts for 341 yards, three touchdowns and no **interceptions**. He had touch and poise and vision. He lofted the ball, and he dumped it off. He was sacked only once. He took what the Cowboys were giving. Which was everything north of the Alamo. Bobby Layne never had a playoff game like this. Hardly any quarterback in history has.

Kramer deserved his praise—and then some—but it should be remembered that it was the threat of Sanders that allowed him to make so many completions; Dallas defenders were so keyed on stopping Sanders that they could not cover all the Lions receivers. Sanders was contained in the first half by an aggressive Dallas defense, but he broke through in the fourth quarter with a spectacular 47-yard touchdown run. Asked by *Sports Illustrated* what allowed him to do this, Sanders replied: "After the guy hit me, I was still on my feet. That was pretty much it." The article continued, "Right. And the Mona Lisa's a cartoon." The final score was 38-6.

JIM AND BARRY

Two great running backs could hardly be less alike. One used strength and sheer grit, in a time when blacks had to earn every yard through heroic effort. The other employed grace, balance, symmetry, and speed in an era in which the majority of NFL players was black. None of this is meant to elevate Jim Brown, to downplay Barry Sanders, or the reverse. When it comes to greatness, people want to compare.

Born on St. Simons Island in Georgia in 1936, Jim Brown came north at an early age, played college ball, and then played his entire NFL career with the Cleveland Browns. In nine years with the team, Brown gained 12,312 yards for an average of 5.2 yards per carry (he also scored 106 touchdowns). The statistics alone, though, do not suffice to explain the man and his impact.

Intensely prideful, Brown used a brooding manner and a forward run that simply bowled over opponents. In a time like ours—saturated with sports drinks and energy bars—it is hard to imagine that Brown purposely chose never to drink water

Pundits marveled at the Lions' performance against Dallas, but they pointed—correctly—to the painful fact that Detroit had never beaten the Washington Redskins, the next opponent, at RFK Stadium in the nation's capital. Not once.

The Redskins were the same powerhouse that had dumped the Lions, brutally, on the opening day of the 1991 season. The Lions came in with more confidence than they had possessed in a decade, but all their hopes were blasted by Washington's

during games: Whether he thought this made him tougher or if it was just part of his image is difficult to say.

Brown experienced plenty of racial discrimination during his nine NFL years. Much of it, though, was anger at how good he was and how difficult he was to stop. There were some nasty moments at the line of scrimmage and in piles of players, but Brown always got up and kept going. When he retired, in 1966, he had set a standard by which all future running backs would be measured.

Sanders never faced as much racial discrimination: He faced size discrimination. Ever since he was in grade school, coaches had refrained from using him, saying he was too small. Sanders proved them wrong, again and again. Perhaps Sanders knew he was luckier than Brown—that he had less outright discrimination to endure—and he always had a voice whispering in his ear. William Sanders, Barry's father, continually told family, friends, and anyone who would listen that Jim Brown was a man among boys, the greatest running back of them all.

It was a good thing that Barry was not the competitive type.

Glancing upfield, Barry Sanders looked for room to run against the Dallas Cowboys during a playoff game on January 5, 1992. Lions quarterback Erik Kramer had a great day, passing for three touchdowns, mainly because the Dallas defense was focused on trying to contain Sanders. Detroit handily won the game, 38-6.

offensive line. As *Sports Illustrated* put it, referring to the nickname of the Redskins' offensive line, "Hail to the Hogs."

Kramer, who had been so sensational against the Dallas Cowboys, could not get going against the Redskins. His first pass of the day was batted away; hit hard by the defense, he **fumbled** on the second; and it was 7-0 Redskins with a little more than one minute played in the game. The Lions' fortunes only went downhill from there, as they were thrashed 41-10.

Sanders had a subpar day. Through the last five games of the regular season, he had outmaneuvered and just plain embarrassed defensive units, but the Redskins were ready for him. He had 44 yards on 11 carries that day.

And so the Miracle Season of 1991, the "Thumbs Up" season dedicated to Mike Utley, came to a painful close at RFK Stadium. But Lions fans were greatly encouraged by what their team had done in 1991, and there were high hopes for 1992.

And Sanders? He, too, had endured a difficult year. His sister Nancy died in November, the same month that Utley was carried off the field. Sanders finished second in the race for the NFL rushing title, with 1,548 yards, but he was frustrated that all his hard work—and that of the team—had crashed to an end in January.

ENVISIONING GREATNESS

By the summer of 1992, Sanders was already considered one of the great running backs of NFL history. He dodged better, ran faster, and piled up more yards than almost anyone else, except Emmitt Smith of the Dallas Cowboys. Years later, when writing his autobiography, Sanders described the source of his motivation on the field:

> Anyone who has ever done anything astounding started out with a vision of what he or she wanted to create. That vision begins with a picture you play over and over in your mind. For me, the vision formed on fall Saturday afternoons while watching Tony Dorsett, the University of Pittsburgh's amazing running back, pierce the line and rocket down the sideline. It formed on Sunday afternoons when I saw Marcus Allen gliding like a figure skater over the turf.

Sanders's fans—their number was growing all the time—thought he was already in the all-time class of great running backs, but they also knew that he had to stick around many years to fully prove it. What, after all, had made Walter Payton the greatest of them all, with more than 16,000 lifetime rushing yards? The fact he played for more than a decade? What allowed Eric Dickerson to become the second running back to get more than 15,000 yards from scrimmage? The same thing. Sanders's admirers, and the man himself, knew he had to stay healthy and fit for a long time in order to ensure his place in the NFL history books.

In *The Physics of Football*, published in 2005, Timothy Gay explained Sanders's amazing success in more technical terms:

> Perhaps no one has ever juked [made rapid changes in direction] better than Barry Sanders of the Detroit Lions (although others might bestow that honor on Walter Payton). Consider the common scenario of Sanders squirting through a hole his offensive line has opened and squaring off with a waiting **linebacker**. Sanders's velocity vector through the line is roughly straight ahead with a magnitude (length) of 18 feet per second. . . . Sanders plants his right foot hard just as a head-on collision with the defender seems to be inevitable, and, literally, in the blink of an eye, he is now moving at 18 feet per second at right angles to his initial velocity. . . . The hapless linebacker's reaction to this juke move is typical of defensive players who encountered Sanders in the open field: He crumples like a pile of wilted sweat socks.

Of course there was a price for this style of play. Using Newton's Second Law, Timothy Gay calculated that Sanders exerted 880 pounds (399 kilograms) of pressure on the ground to make that juke (or turn) and all 880 pounds slid through

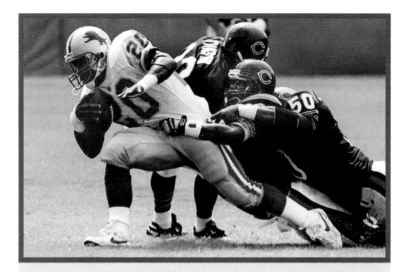

During a play in the season opener in 1992, Barry Sanders dragged three Chicago defenders as he pushed to gain more yardage. Sanders ran for 104 yards that day, but the Lions lost 27-24—a portent of the season ahead.

Sanders's knees and ankles. It was remarkable that he was not injured more often.

And so Sanders changed. Not all at once, but he made steps to improve his diet and overall fitness. Early in his career, Sanders was renowned for devouring Dove and Snickers bars, for demolishing two to three helpings at a meal. His appetite remained strong, but he shifted to salads and white meat, with noticeable results.

1992

Sanders's fourth NFL season began with high hopes among the Detroit Lions. Their remarkable late-season burst of the previous years convinced them that they could go all the way in 1992. The season, though, began with an agonizing loss to the Chicago Bears, 27-24. Sanders had 104 yards rushing that day, but it was not enough to win the day.

One week later, on September 13, Sanders and the Lions had a satisfying victory over the Minnesota Vikings, 31-17.

Then the Lions met the Washington Redskins who, once again, proved too tough, 13-10.

Rodney Peete had been out with an injury during the last third of the 1991 season, but he was back with a vengeance, throwing for a career-high 323 passing yards against Tampa Bay on September 27: Unfortunately, the team did not cash in on Peete's sterling performance, as the Lions lost 27-23. When the Lions lost to the New Orleans Saints 13-7 and then to the Minnesota Vikings 31-14, the team that had come one game short of the Super Bowl the year before was now 1–5.

Detroit rebounded, beating Tampa Bay 38-7 on a day that saw Sanders rush for 122 yards, but the Lions lost to Green Bay the following week, 27-13. The team sank to its nadir in the middle of November, losing to the Dallas Cowboys 37-3 and to the Pittsburgh Steelers 17-14. Commentators noted that a team that worked as hard as the Detroit Lions should not be 2–8 at this point in the season.

Finally came a measure of validation; on November 22, the Lions edged the Cincinnati Bengals 19-13. Sanders rushed for 151 yards that day, his best performance of the year. Two more losses followed, as the Houston Oilers dumped the Lions 24-21 and the Green Bay Packers took them down 38-10, but the Lions rose up for the last part of the season, beating Cleveland 24-14 and the Chicago Bears 16-3. The season closed with a loss to the San Francisco 49ers, 24-6, but at least some pride had been restored.

Sanders seldom had anything to say about his team's defeats. When asked, he would shrug and say that the opposing team had been good that day. But when the final statistics and numbers came in, the Lions were 5–11 for the year, tied for last in the NFC Central Division. The team *had* to get better.

Nineties Football

Every sports decade has its admirers and its detractors. Every decade since the appearance of television has had millions of fans weigh in with their own opinions. On one view most would agree: The 1990s were a decade of great change in professional football.

THE SEARCH FOR PARITY

Beginning in the late 1980s, the NFL commissioner, Paul Tagliabue, and his advisers began to work for "parity," or rough equality, among the then 28 teams of the NFL. Tagliabue and his staff were convinced that dynasties were bad for the game, that fans would tire of watching the same teams win their divisions year after year. The point could certainly be argued; very few people had tired of the Green Bay Packers in the 1960s or the Pittsburgh Steelers of the late 1970s. But Tagliabue had the whip hand, and by the mid-1990s his vision of parity was beginning to prevail.

One dynasty did emerge from the pack, however; the Dallas Cowboys went on a wild tear in the mid-1990s, winning three Super Bowls to add to the two won by Tom Landry's team back in the 1970s. But most of the numbers, if not the magic, belonged to the notion of parity; the **salary cap** alone made it difficult for one team to rule the roost.

One might think that the salary cap and the quest for parity would benefit the Detroit Lions, but their up-and-down performance (12–4 in 1991 and 5–11 in 1992) hurt their chances. Draft picks went first to the team with the previous year's worst record, so sometimes the Lions chose high in the draft and sometimes they were far down. If the Lions had anything going for them, it was the offensive threat of Barry Sanders. But for how long?

1993 SEASON

Sanders's fifth NFL season started off with a bang. The Lions defeated the Atlanta Falcons on opening day 30-13, and then edged the New England Patriots by 19-16, a day on which Sanders racked up 148 yards. The third week saw an embarrassing loss to the New Orleans Saints, 14-3, but the Lions roared back in Week 4, beating the Phoenix Cardinals by 26-20.

There followed a painful loss to Tampa Bay, 27-10, despite 130 rushing yards from Sanders. But the Lions got on a winning track on October 17, beating the Seattle Seahawks 30-10. Sanders rushed for 101 yards that day, putting him near the top of NFL runners at Week 6. From there it was on to a victory over the Los Angeles Rams, 16-13, and a narrow 30-27 win over the Minnesota Vikings. Halfway through the season, the Lions were 6–2, equal to their start in 1991.

Sanders excelled during a fine win over Tampa Bay on November 7. The Lions prevailed 23-0, and Sanders rushed for

187 yards (it's hard to say why, but Sanders often had his big-number days when playing against Tampa Bay). Detroit lost to Green Bay 26-17 on November 21. Though no one knew it at the time, Green Bay was about to found a new dynasty, built on the broad shoulders and thick hands of Brett Favre (he would later be called the "Iron Man" of the NFL). Detroit lost its Thanksgiving Day game to the Chicago Bears, 10-6, and lost Sanders for the rest of the regular season, after he left the game with a knee injury in the third quarter. When Minnesota shut out Detroit on December 5, it seemed that the early-season magic was gone.

The Lions came back during much of the last stretch of the season, however. They beat Phoenix 21-14; fell to San Francisco 55-17; and then defeated the Chicago Bears 20-14 and Green Bay, on January 2, 1994, by 10 points. The regular season ended on a high note, as the Lions finished with a 10–6 record, tops in the NFC Central. After missing the last five games of the season, Sanders finished with only 1,115 rushing yards and a scant three touchdowns. But, like all of the other Lions, he was delighted to be in the playoffs, and he would be back from his injury.

POSTSEASON

In the **wild card** game of the NFC, the Lions faced the Green Bay Packers. Both teams knew and understood the other's method of play, and both coaches felt they had the edge going into the contest. What emerged on that January day was a truism, at least for the moment: A superb quarterback will find a way to win.

Brett Favre threw and ran, scrambled and passed, and Green Bay took home the victory, even with 169 rushing yards for Sanders. It was a sour loss for the Lions, who had beaten Green Bay just two weeks earlier, and yet another disappointment for coach Wayne Fontes and team owner William Clay Ford. The Lions went to the sidelines, or rather to their home TV sets, and watched Dallas walk off with the Super Bowl.

Barry Sanders bounced outside to find some running room during the Lions' NFC wild-card playoff game against the Green Bay Packers on January 8, 1994. Despite Sanders's 169 rushing yards, Green Bay prevailed 28-24.

1994 SEASON

With 120 rushing yards against the Atlanta Falcons, Sanders started his sixth NFL season well. Detroit narrowly won the game, 31-28.

One week later, Detroit lost to the Minnesota Vikings 10-3. But then followed one of Sanders's best NFL games to date. He rushed for 194 yards against the Dallas Cowboys, and the Lions won 20-17. A week later he rushed for 131 yards in a loss to the New England Patriots, 23-17. Though the Lions lost, Sanders added to his growing legend that day, by running three times around one defender in the course of making a 37-yard run. One Sunday after that came another remarkable performance, one that the columnists called the "Barry Sanders Sock Hop."

The Lions had the ball on their own 10-yard line in a game that was, typically, tight and close. Sanders was handed the ball and he got almost, but not quite, through the line

CHASTITY AND CHILDBIRTH

Barry Sanders had long been a poster boy for all that was good in the NFL. At a time when athletes were suspected of all sorts of wrongdoing, including the use of performance-enhancing drugs (steroids), he had been a model player. In January 1992, as Detroit won its first playoff game in decades, Sanders was featured on the back cover of *Sports Illustrated*, the place usually reserved for Marlboro Man advertising. Sweat glistening, Sanders advertised a pair of running shoes, but his message seemed broader than athletic wear:

> Too often we are scared.
> Scared of what we might not be able to do
> Scared of what people might think if we tried
> We let our fears stand in the way of our hopes.

There was no doubt that Sanders had not let fear stand in his way, and he was indeed a fine model for young people. Therefore, it came as a shock to many to learn that Sanders had fathered a child (he had previously done a public service announcement for chastity prior to marriage) in 1994.

Sanders did not marry the woman who gave birth to his son. He was quiet and calm in talking to newspaper reporters, telling them that his infant son was healthy and happy, and that was all that mattered.

of scrimmage, when Tampa Bay **safety** Tony Bouie wrapped a hand around Sanders's left ankle. The two struggled for a second, and then Sanders broke free, leaving his left shoe in the other man's hands! Accelerating in that way only he could, Sanders burst down the field, making it to the Tampa 5-yard line. Those watching simply gasped; Sanders was faster with one shoe off than most people were with both shoes on. In *The 100 Best Plays of Football History*, author Jonathan Rand placed Sanders's sock hop at No. 56.

On another play in the game against Tampa Bay, Sanders had an 85-yard run. Yet all his theatrics were for naught as the Lions lost 24-14. People were beginning to ask: What good was it for Sanders to run for such incredible yardage when the Detroit defense seemed unable to contain its opponents?

One more painful loss followed, on October 9, to the San Francisco 49ers, a team that Detroit seldom, if ever, beat. After a **bye week**, the Lions beat the Chicago Bears 21-16 (Sanders had 167 rushing yards), followed by a win over the New York Giants 28-25 (this time Sanders had 146 yards). At the season's halfway point, Detroit was 4–4.

The Green Bay Packers spoiled the Lions' two-game streak with a 38-30 victory, but Detroit's season finally turned the corner on November 13. Sanders rushed for 237 yards—his personal best and one of the best running days for any back ever—as Detroit beat Tampa Bay 14-9. After a 20-10 loss to Chicago, the Lions defeated Buffalo 35-21 in the Thanksgiving Day game. The victory was a result of the strong arm and exceptional sight of quarterback Dave Krieg, who had 351 passing yards. Sweetest of all was turning the tables on Green Bay, defeating the Packers 34-31 on December 4. Sanders had another stellar game, rushing for 188 yards on 20 carries. By now, the Lions were back in contention for the playoffs.

Detroit met and mastered the New York Jets 18-7 on December 10, then enjoyed a 41-19 runaway game in which they pasted the Minnesota Vikings. The season's final game

All alone, Barry Sanders sped toward the end zone during a 64-yard touchdown run against the Minnesota Vikings on December 17, 1994. Sanders finished the season as the league's No. 1 rusher, with 1,883 yards. The Lions, though, stumbled again in the first round of the playoffs.

fell on Sunday, Christmas Day, and it was Miami that got the gift, beating Detroit 27-20. Still, the Lions had rebounded to a 9–7 record, good enough to finish in a three-way tie for second place in the NFC Central Division and good enough for a wild-card spot in the postseason.

PLAYOFFS

In the first round, the Lions faced the Green Bay Packers on the last day of 1994. *The New York Times* described the excitement:

> They have played each other in 64 consecutive years. They have met five times in this calendar year. This

time, the game breaker came with 1 minute 45 seconds left at historic Lambeau Field. Detroit trailed Green Bay by 16-10 and had the ball at the Packers' 17-yard line. **Fourth down**. Thirteen yards to go for a first down.

Detroit quarterback Dave Krieg lofted a fine ball to the end zone. No. 84, Herman Moore, snagged it, but he landed out of the end zone. Just out. Green Bay got the ball back, and on that possession, the Packers took a safety. Final result: Packers 16, Lions 12. But there was a much more astonishing number: Barry Sanders, who gave his all, gained -1 yard for the day. The *Times* put it like this:

> Yesterday the Lions and 58,125 Packers parishioners kept waiting for him to break that long one, but he never did. Never came close. Usually he makes the first tackler miss and twice he was out near the sideline one-on-one with Wayne Simmons, but twice the Packers' outside linebacker nailed him to the green-painted dirt.

Of course there were other statistics from the 1994 season. How about 1,883 rushing yards, best in the NFL? How about 8,672, Sanders's total rushing yards to date? Still, -1 was a hard number for Sanders and the Lions to take.

Ho-Hum

Barry Sanders never described any game, season, or year of his NFL career as "ho-hum," but many a Detroit Lions fan did. The Lions seemed to find new ways to lose, the home crowd said.

1995 SEASON

Sanders's seventh NFL season began with the Lions facing the Pittsburgh Steelers, who would go on to be the AFC champions that season. Sanders rushed for 108 yards that day, but the Lions lost 23-20.

Then came a matchup against the Minnesota Vikings. Sometime during the 1990s, the idea that Detroit was doomed to lose to Minnesota had disappeared—the jinx seemed gone— but on this occasion the Vikings prevailed 20-10. When the

Arizona Cardinals beat Detroit in Week 3, 20-17, the Lions were in a 0–3 hole.

An appearance on *Monday Night Football*, on September 25, boosted everyone's spirits. The Lions did not get many Monday night games over the years, but they savored this one with a rare defeat of the San Francisco 49ers, 27-24. Given the trail of losses to San Francisco, this was one of the sweetest victories of the 1995 season. From there, the Lions went on to beat Cleveland 38-20 in a game that saw Sanders gain 157 yards. But, as happened so often in the past, the Lions came up short against the Green Bay Packers, losing 30-21. Sanders had a fine day rushing, piling up 124 yards, but Brett Favre had an even better one, passing for 342.

The Washington Redskins inflicted another of their routine beatings on the Lions, 36-30, and then came sweet revenge, with the Lions beating the Packers 24-16. Sanders had 167 rushing yards in one of his better performances: Even Favre could not beat the Lions this time. But, with the season half over, Detroit stood at 3–5.

Detroit fell to the Atlanta Falcons on November 5, by 34-22. The Lions rebounded with a good win over Tampa Bay, 27-24, and then, on November 19, Sanders had a 120-yard day as the Lions beat the Chicago Bears 24-17. The real heroics, and histrionics, though, were saved for a wild shootout on Thanksgiving Day.

Turkey Day matched the Lions against the Minnesota Vikings. Both sides—and virtually every player—gave their flat-out best effort (Sanders rushed for 138 yards, Herman Moore had 127 receiving yards, and quarterback Scott Mitchell passed for 410) in a high-scoring 44-38 victory for Detroit. This was one of the most satisfying Thanksgiving Days the Lions had ever enjoyed.

Ten days later, the Lions made another appearance on *Monday Night Football*, this time against the Chicago Bears. Detroit's defense did its work and then some, as the Lions won

During a photo shoot in the 1990s, Barry Sanders appeared in the Lions' locker room at the Silverdome. Sanders finished the 1995 season with 1,500 rushing yards, but his per-carry average had fallen from the previous season. He was aware that time was now an opponent, too.

27-7. From there, the Lions went from glory to glory, beating Houston 24-17, thrashing Jacksonville 44-0, and beating Tampa Bay on the last day of the regular season, 37-10. As in the past, the Lions proved much more dangerous in the last four or five games of the season than in the first.

Sanders ended the season with 1,500 yards on the nose, 11 touchdowns, and a per-carry average of 4.8 yards. Good as that was, some critics began to murmur that he was going downhill (his per-carry average had been 5.7 the year before). Sanders was as aware as anyone that history—the passing of each year—was against him. Great running backs—even the greatest—tended to fade at a certain point (often around the age of 29) and never recover.

NO GUARANTEES

Detroit played well enough in the last part of the season to reach the playoffs. Their first opponent would be the Philadelphia Eagles, who, coincidentally, had former Detroit Lion Rodney Peete as their quarterback. In the days leading up to the game, Detroit offensive tackle Lomas Brown made some boastful statements about how the Lions would win—he guaranteed it—and that it was just a matter of whether his team would steamroll the Eagles early or take their time. Eagles head coach Ray Rhodes took newspaper clippings of Brown's statements and pinned them up in his team's locker room so all the players could learn what the Lions thought of them.

Game day was December 30, 1995, in Philadelphia. The Lions came out with all hope and expectation, but they ran smack into one of their former teammate's best performances. Peete was sensational, throwing for three touchdowns while going 17 of 25 for 270 yards. The Lions suffered by comparison; they had six interceptions and one fumble. The game ended with the highest number of points ever scored in an NFL playoff game (95), with the Eagles on top, 58-37. The game was not nearly as close as that score seemed; the Eagles had led by 51-7 at one point.

Lomas Brown had set the Lions up for a painful humiliation.

1996 SEASON

Sanders entered his eighth season with as much motivation as ever. He was well on his way to football immortality, but he wanted his team to reach for, and attain, the golden ring of a Super Bowl.

The season opener was against the Minnesota Vikings who, as usual, found a way to beat the Lions: this time it was 17-13. Sanders, though, piled up 163 yards on the ground. He continued his good start the following week, rushing for 125 yards in a game that saw Detroit beat Tampa Bay 21-6. Detroit stumbled the following week, losing to the Philadelphia Eagles 24-17. Then came a measure of satisfaction, with the Lions beating the Chicago Bears 35-16. And on September 29, Detroit thrashed Tampa Bay 27-0.

Early in October, the Lions beat the Atlanta Falcons 28-24, but that was the last victory for some time. On October 13, Detroit fell to Oakland 37-21; this was followed by a 35-7 shellacking by the New York Giants. Early in November, Sanders had 152 rushing yards against Green Bay, but the Lions still lost 28-18.

On November 11, the Lions made one of their rare appearances on *Monday Night Football.* Sanders and the Lions gave a good effort but went down to the San Diego Chargers 27-21.

The Lions pulled out of their four-game skid on Sunday, November 17, edging the Seattle Seahawks 17-16. Sanders had 134 rushing yards that day. The Lions, though, could not fight off their losing ways, falling the following week to Chicago 31-14. Four days later came the annual Thanksgiving Day game, which pitted the Lions against the Kansas City Chiefs. The two teams had a lot in common; both were generally underdogs on the road but fierce competitors at home. Detroit hosted this game, but it lost a close one, 28-24.

In their next game, the Lions lost another tight one to Minnesota, 24-22, and then were pasted the next week by the Green Bay Packers, the premier team in the NFL at the time, 31-3. Quarterback Brett Favre was having the best season of his life, leading the Packers to glory they had not seen since the 1960s. One more game remained, and on Monday night, December 23, Sanders and the Lions met the San Francisco

Barry Sanders eluded Oakland cornerback James Trapp in the first quarter of the Lions-Raiders game on October 13, 1996. Sanders rushed for only 36 yards in the game, and Detroit lost 37-21—beginning a skid that would see Detroit lose nine out of its last 10 games. After the season was over, the Lions fired coach Wayne Fontes.

49ers, whom they had finally beaten the year before. This time it was a good, well-contested game, but the 49ers prevailed 24-14 (Sanders had 175 yards rushing).

COACHES AND THEIR STYLES

Green Bay Packer coach Vince Lombardi practically symbolized American football in the 1960s; the same could be said of Tom Landry, head coach of the Dallas Cowboys from 1960 to 1988. Their styles could not have been more different; Lombardi was all fire, enthusiasm, and exhortation, while Landry was cerebral and cool, to the point where people thought him cocky. Only later did fans learn that Landry was a devout Christian to whom football—while exciting and challenging—was never the central part of his life.

When Barry Sanders arrived in Detroit in 1989, Wayne Fontes was in his first full year as the Lions' head coach (he had come on board late in the 1988 season). A big, genial man with an expressive face, Fontes became a favorite with his players, whom he treated more as nephews than as sons (one thinks of the stern, taskmaster father and the genial, helpful uncle). For a team struggling to get on its feet and into the playoffs, Fontes was almost the perfect coach: charming, fun, and sociable. As the decade progressed, and as NFL draft picks led to higher hopes for the Lions, Detroit's love affair with Fontes soured: He was too easygoing, people said. *Sports Illustrated* writers agreed, noting that Fontes was the cat with nine lives, the coach who somehow kept his job despite the chaos around him.

Detroit owner William C. Ford finally sacked Fontes at the end of 1996. He left with a 66–67 regular-season record, compiled from 1988 to 1996 (he was 1–4 in the playoffs).

Two years later, Fontes sued the Lions, claiming an injury he sustained while coaching had prevented him from obtaining other work in the NFL. The suit failed.

Detroit ended the year at 5–11, dead last in the NFC Central Division. Three days after the season was over, on the day after Christmas, Lions owner William C. Ford fired head coach Wayne Fontes.

Sanders regretted the departure of Fontes, who, he thought, should have had another chance to prove himself in 1997. But leadership of the team passed to Bobby Ross.

Born in Virginia in 1935, Ross had coached Georgia Tech to a national championship in 1990 and, in five years with the San Diego Chargers, had led them to the playoffs three times. In January 1997, Ford led Ross to the podium to introduce him as a winner, as the man who would make things different for Detroit.

Ross gratefully accepted the praise, then spoke of the need for the Lions to reach the Super Bowl. For every team, he said, that had not reached or won the Super Bowl, there was an empty feeling inside.

Barry Sanders and his teammates could relate to that.

Magic Year

I feel embarrassed talking about how I feel.
—Barry Sanders

As he entered his ninth NFL season, Barry Sanders had a great deal with which to be happy. His individual statistics were very strong, although not quite as grand as that day when he told the Lions assistant coach, "What if I want to gain 2,500 yards?" There was plenty of money in the bank, plenty more coming in, and Sanders had shown that he was good with money: purchasing businesses, increasing the principal, and generally living in a disciplined and responsible manner.

NEW LEADER
Wayne Fontes had been, until now, Sanders's only head coach, but in the winter of 1997, Detroit owner William C. Ford

fired Fontes and hired Bobby Ross. The new coach was quite different in personality and temperament; Fontes had been easygoing—some people called him "soft"—while Ross was driven and intense. He was one of only four coaches to lead a college team to a national title and lead an NFL team to the Super Bowl.

Ross saw—as did most of the fans—that it was no use having Sanders amass sensational yardage if the opposing team was able to do the same against a weak Detroit defense. Therefore, Detroit prepared to defend against the running game, and to make the most of its own stars: Sanders and wide receivers Herman Moore and Johnnie Morton. The "run and shoot" offense was curtailed.

1997 SEASON

The Lions started the season with a matchup against the Atlanta Falcons. Detroit won the game, 28-17, but Sanders had one of his poorest performances to date, rushing for only 33 yards on 15 carries. Was he having trouble adjusting to the new system instituted by Ross?

One week later, Sanders rushed for only 20 yards against Tampa Bay, though he did have 102 receiving yards. Those receptions should, by rights, have made all the difference, but Detroit lost the game 24-17. Now the critics weighed in, charging that the new, more-scaled-back offense created by Ross had "ruined" Sanders, taking away his genius for the run. We do not know if Ross made any new adjustments for the season's third game, but there was a new Sanders, for sure.

Sanders rushed for 161 yards against the Chicago Bears at Soldier Field, helping his team to win 32-7, one of its most convincing performances ever against the Bears. There was nothing an observer could pinpoint, nothing that seemed to say that a new Sanders had been unleashed, but he was about to go on one of the greatest rampages ever known in the game.

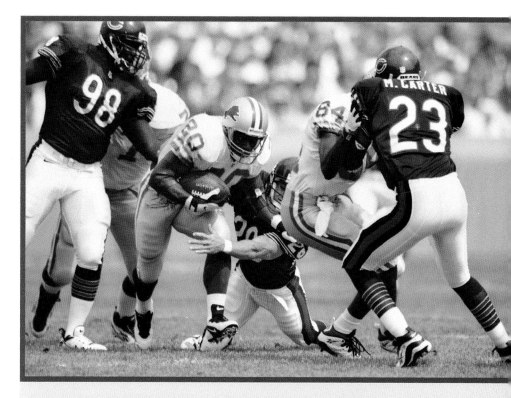

A Chicago Bears defender took down Barry Sanders during a game on September 14, 1997. In the first two games of the season, Sanders rushed for only 53 yards, and many wondered if new coach Bobby Ross's system was stifling Sanders. Against the Bears, Sanders exploded for 161 yards—the beginning of what would be a special season.

Sanders rushed for 113 yards against the New Orleans Saints, but it was not enough to prevent a 35-17 loss. Then the Green Bay Packers, who had created so much frustration for the Lions over the years, came to town. Sanders gained 139 yards in Game 5, as the Lions beat the Packers 26-15. By now, people were taking notice of Sanders's performance; he seemed to have injected new life into his already famous style.

Next came the Buffalo Bills, a team Sanders had always held in high regard, partly because his old Oklahoma State teammate, Thurman Thomas, played there. Sanders rushed for 107 yards that day, but Detroit dropped the game, 22-13. Then came a game against Tampa Bay, played at the Big Sombrero—as the Bucs' stadium was affectionately known—on a brilliant, sunny day.

Tampa Bay, the hottest team in the NFL, had an eight-game winning streak at home; much of this was due to the tireless work of coach Tony Dungy, one of the masters of defensive strategy. But nothing could stop Sanders on this day.

Remembering that Tampa had held him to only 20 yards in the season's second game, Sanders picked his moments well. First he exploded for an 80-yard touchdown run, his longest professional one to date (of course he might have remembered his 100-yard kickoff returns at Oklahoma State University). Not long after, he rushed for an 82-yard touchdown, and in so doing, became the first NFL player ever to rush for two touchdowns of 80 yards or more in the same game. Not long after that, he caught a seven-yard touchdown pass from quarterback Scott Mitchell.

To say that Sanders was the MVP of this particular game is an understatement. He led his team to a convincing 27-9 victory, and, in the process, he passed his father's football idol, Jim Brown, on the all-time rushing-yards list. As of this day, which he ended with 12,513 career yards, Sanders trailed only Tony Dorsett, Eric Dickerson, and Walter Payton, in that order. The big story was how Sanders faked out defenders, ran circles around them, and generally played as if he were a man of 18 instead of 29.

Lots of attention now came Sanders's way, with plenty of pundits asking questions about whether he was the greatest, the fastest, and so forth. Sanders refused to fuel the speculation, saying that he did his best every day and that some days it was good and some days it was not. He failed to add that there were some days when it was just plain out-of-sight!

"It's just good to know that I've succeeded with my team," Sanders said in one interview after the game. "That's all the (recognition) I need."

Sanders had an average day—for him—against the New York Giants, rushing for 105 yards. The Lions lost the game 26-20, and, at midseason they stood at 4–4—the same as in 1996.

After a bye week, the Lions played at Green Bay, and in the early November weather, the Packers prevailed 20-10. Sanders had another 105-yard day, keeping his streak of 100-plus yard games alive, with seven straight. Then came the Washington Redskins, who, true to form, pasted the Lions 30-7 in a game that saw Sanders rush for the same number: 105 yet again. The Lions were now 0–18 against Washington in RFK Stadium. Detroit's hopes of making the playoffs were fading with each Sunday afternoon.

Sanders finally pushed past his 105-yard streak with a 108-yard performance against the Minnesota Vikings. Detroit won 38-15, keeping its playoff hopes alive. But the next week, Sunday, November 23, would go down as one of the all-time "great" days for Barry Sanders.

Playing the Indianapolis Colts—the old team of rusher Eric Dickerson—Sanders powered for 216 yards, including an 80-yard touchdown run. The Lions won 32-10. Sanders became the first NFL running back to rush for more than 100 yards in 10 consecutive games in one season, and he was the first running back to score three touchdowns on runs of 80 yards or more in a season. As he kept churning out the yards, Sanders was seen as having a chance, however small, of gaining 2,000 yards in a season, an accomplishment that had occurred only twice in NFL history: by O.J. Simpson in 1973 and by Dickerson in 1984.

Sanders continued to fend off questions about his place in NFL history. Competing against numbers, he said, was something to which he could not relate. But as the season wore on, and as Detroit's playoff hopes—however slim—continued, Sanders picked up his already stellar performance.

He rushed for 167 yards on Thanksgiving Day, in a game that saw the Lions thrash the Chicago Bears 55-20, setting a franchise record for most points scored. Late in the game,

Barry Sanders raced down the sideline for an 80-yard touchdown run against the Indianapolis Colts on November 23, 1997. He gained 216 yards against the Colts. Earlier in the season, Sanders had touchdown runs of 80 and 82 yards against the Tampa Bay Buccaneers. Some were beginning to wonder if Sanders would rush for more than 2,000 yards for the season.

Sanders passed Dickerson on the all-time rushing list, leaving only one man—the great Walter Payton—still in the lead with 16,726 career yards. The following week, Sanders gained 137 yards against the Miami Dolphins, on a day when the Lions came terribly close but lost at the end 33-30.

Across the league, it was turning out to be a great year for running backs. *Sports Illustrated* noted that: "Only two players, O.J. Simpson and Eric Dickerson, have run for 2,000 yards in a season. With two games left, the NFL's three best backs have a shot. Barry Sanders needs 269 yards, Terrell Davis [of the Denver Broncos] 278, and Jerome Bettis needs 415 to hit the mark."

On December 14, Sanders continued his march toward the 2,000-yard mark, rushing for 138 yards and playing a big part in what Ross called the best comeback he had ever had the privilege of coaching, a 14-13 defeat of the Minnesota Vikings. The Lions were now 8–7, and their slim, one-point victory kept their playoff ambitions alive for one more week.

The Lions and the New York Jets both entered Game 16 with apprehension. The team that won would make the play-offs; the team that lost would go home for the year. *The New York Times* expressed it best: "Sanders and a Foiled Option Pass End a Turnaround Season."

The Jets, coached by the legendary Bill Parcells, were in a rebuilding year. Detroit, coached by Bobby Ross, was in a make-or-break one. The Jets contained Sanders beautifully in the first half, but he broke out on the last play of the third quarter, with a 47-yard run to the Jets' 17-yard line. He scored a touchdown three plays later. The Jets made a strong comeback toward the end of the fourth quarter, but the Lions held them off, and Sanders made a totally unsensational two-yard run that gave him exactly 2,000 yards for the season. The crowd went wild.

Yet his joy—and that of his teammates—was diluted.

Over the years, Sanders had been fortunate when it came to injuries: He had few to record. But he had seen Mike Utley carried off the field in 1991, and this day he and everyone else on the field watched linebacker Reggie Brown collapse after what should have been a routine tackle. Brown stopped breathing.

For 15 minutes, the two teams and the crowd kept very quiet while first-aid responders gave mouth-to-mouth resuscitation to Brown. People kept hoping he would get up and walk off "on his own power," but that never happened. Instead, Brown, who suffered a spinal-cord contusion, was carried off; though he made a full recovery, he had played his last NFL game.

When the game was over and people asked Sanders how he felt about compiling 2,053 yards for the season (he had two more runs after the "big" one), he replied, "I feel embarrassed talking about how I feel." Reporters then asked Jets coach Bill Parcells what he felt, and his response was: "My feelings are really insignificant compared to the feeling for that young man who got hurt."

Not only were the Lions going to the playoffs, but Sanders had ended the regular season with 2,053 rushing yards, a bit ahead of O.J. Simpson (2,003) and a bit behind Eric Dickerson (2,105).

Critics could—and do—point out that Simpson rushed for 2,000-plus yards at a time when the NFL season was 14 games, not 16. They point out that Sanders's great rushing attempts came at a time when the NFL game was different from what it was in the past. There is no disputing the accuracy of these claims. The game of 1997 was different from that of 1984 and that of 1973. But one has to look at many factors when assessing greatness, and, as a *Sports Illustrated* writer put it, "No one has done it with less help." Throughout his career, Sanders did not have great run blockers to assist him. Time and again, he generated the offensive power in his legs, moved in, around, and past defenders, and created scoring opportunities for the Detroit Lions.

POSTSEASON

The NFC wild-card game was between the Lions and their perennial foe, the Tampa Bay Buccaneers. Most observers called this game a toss-up, since neither team had enjoyed a great year (Sanders's running was Detroit's big standout), but they should have paid more attention to the defensive game

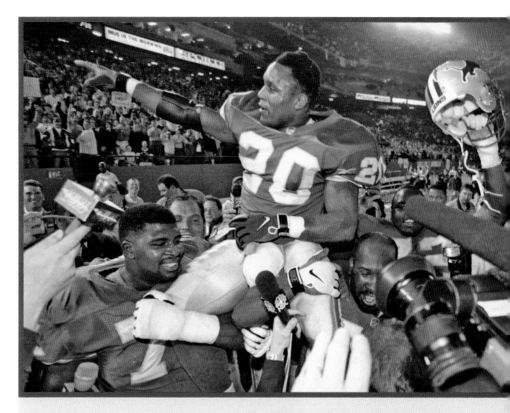

Fellow Lions carried Barry Sanders around the field after he rushed for 184 yards in the 1997 season finale against the New York Jets—giving him 2,053 yards for the year. Sanders also scored the winning touchdown, and with the victory, the Lions were headed for the playoffs.

on both sides. Defensive coach Tony Dungy of Tampa Bay was quietly—oh so quietly—becoming the best in the business. A former Pittsburgh Steeler, he was one of the first African Americans to work his way up in the coaching ranks (later he became the first black head coach to win a Super Bowl). On game day, Dungy rolled out all sorts of tricks to smother the Detroit Lions offense, and many of them succeeded.

Game day was December 28, 1997. Tampa was hosting its first playoff game in 18 years. The two teams had split their regular-season meetings.

The Lions struggled throughout the game. Sanders was held to only 65 yards on 18 carries. Quarterback Scott Mitchell was carried off the field on a stretcher after an injury sustained in the last few seconds of the third quarter. Fans and teammates alike held their breath, dreading that his injury might be as severe as Reggie Brown's just one week earlier (Mitchell, who had a mild concussion, recovered quickly). The overall result: The Lions lost 20-10.

Tampa Bay went on to get smothered by the Green Bay Packers in an NFC divisional playoff game, 21-7, but that was cold comfort to the Lions, who went home with nothing but a pocketful of dashed hopes.

REST FOR THE WEARY

By the spring of 1998, Sanders was showing signs of age. It was not apparent on the field but rather in person. Rushing for all those yards against formidable defenses had taken their toll.

He was at a turning point in life. Certainly he could strive for more, aim his sights at displacing Walter Payton as the all-time leader in rushing yards. He was slightly less than 3,000 yards behind Payton. Certainly he could fight with his beloved team for yet another try at the playoffs and that elusive Super Bowl ring. But Sanders knew the odds were tough. As he approached his thirtieth birthday, in July 1998, he knew that few running backs had been able to continue their great performances after the age of 29, much less 30. Still, he was in the running for another season.

1998 NFL SEASON

Sanders started his tenth NFL season without some beloved figures from previous years. One of his best friends on the Lions, **center** Kevin Glover, was traded to the Seattle Seahawks. Why, Sanders wondered?

There were still standouts, like receiver Herman Moore and the up-and-coming Johnnie Morton, but Sanders missed the camaraderie of former seasons. The lack of cohesion showed on opening day, when the Lions were dumped 38-19 by the Green Bay Packers.

BARRY AND "SWEETNESS"

Running back Walter Payton of the Chicago Bears was one of the most beloved figures in American sports. Bursting onto the scene in the late 1970s, he practically ate up yardage during the early and mid-1980s. Like Barry Sanders, Payton was relatively small, 5 feet 10 inches (178 centimeters), and also like Sanders, he possessed enormous heart. Where Sanders was the master at finding a way around defensive linemen, Payton was the best at knocking through them: He was immensely strong and fast.

Early in Sanders's career, sometime during the 1990 season, Payton watched him play against the Bears and, when asked to comment, he replied, "I don't think I was ever *that* good." Payton fans and Sanders fans could debate that ad infinitum, but what mattered was the expression of mutual respect; whenever he was asked to comment on his skill relative to people like Payton, Sanders would shrug and say he had a hard time competing against people he had idolized in his youth (that went for Billy Sims, Marcus Allen, Tony Dorsett, and, of course, Payton).

In February 1999, Payton revealed to the media that he had a rare liver disease and that he did not expect to live much longer. There was an enormous outpouring of affection and support from his many fans, and, as the 1999 season approached, Sanders may have turned the thought over in his mind: Did he wish to try to surpass the all-time rushing record held by a man in the throes of death?

Walter Payton died in November 1999, at the age of 45.

Barry Sanders sat in the end zone during the Lions' game against the San Francisco 49ers on December 14, 1998. The Lions were in the midst of a four-game losing streak at the end of the season. Perhaps Sanders was beginning to wonder if this would be his last year in the NFL.

Game 2 saw Sanders rush for 185 yards, showing that the magic had not disappeared from his incredible, twisting legs. But Detroit lost the game to Cincinnati 34-28.

In the third week, coach Bobby Ross put in Charlie Batch, picked by the Lions in the second round of that year's draft, as the new starting quarterback. Tall, rangy, and possessing a commanding arm, Batch seemed just the ticket to improve the Lions' chances that season. Although the Lions lost the third game, 29-6, to the Minnesota Vikings, Detroit won Game 4, over Tampa Bay, by 27-6, on *Monday Night Football* with Batch at the helm. Sanders had 131 rushing yards that evening. A disappointing 31-27 loss to the Chicago Bears followed, but Sanders and the Lions saved some special magic for a rematch with the Green Bay Packers.

On Thursday, October 15, Sanders had 155 rushing yards, including a 73-yard touchdown run, which helped his team to beat Green Bay 27-20. This was the best win of the season so far, coming over the team that had won the Super Bowl two seasons before and had been the runner-up the previous year. The season, though, went downhill from there.

Detroit lost to the Minnesota Vikings on October 25, 34-13, and to the Arizona Cardinals 17-15 a week later. Despite Sanders's rushing for 140 yards, the Lions lost to the Philadelphia Eagles 10-9 in early November. The Lions gained some measure of revenge, by beating the Chicago Bears 26-3, and by taking down Tampa Bay 28-25: This was done against what was then the best defense in the NFL. There was one more win, a 19-16 defeat of the Pittsburgh Steelers on Thanksgiving Day, but from then on it was only losses, with Detroit falling to Jacksonville 37-22, San Francisco 35-13, the Atlanta Falcons 24-17, and finally to the Baltimore Ravens 19-10. Years later, Sanders described his feelings in his autobiography:

> We were playing in Baltimore against the Ravens on a raw, rainy afternoon in December of 1998. During my career I rarely fumbled, but I had uncharacteristically let the ball—and the game—slip through my fingers. Also uncharacteristically, the guy who never exploded in celebration when crossing the goal line, the guy who kept his emotions tucked away as tightly as he tucked away the football, cried in front of several teammates in the locker room.
>
> An era was coming to an end.

A New Life

I'd been running on fumes for years.
—Barry Sanders

Change usually is not sudden. Even when we experience something as huge, full of impact for our lives, it usually has built over a period of time, attracting little notice till the moment when something breaks, snaps, or changes course. So it was with Barry Sanders's NFL career.

THE MAGIC IS GONE
During the winter and spring of 1999, Sanders had little communication with his teammates or with the coaching staff, led by Bobby Ross. This was not unusual. Sanders was never a big "talker" and many an off-season had seen him travel,

spend time with his family, or simply rest quietly at home. But as spring turned to summer, the silence from Sanders's end started to become ominous.

Ross tried to contact Sanders as many as 13 times by letter and telephone, but he received no reply. Other teammates picked up the phone but found Sanders out or away. And then, just as Lions players were about to come together for summer training camp, someone from the team picked up a strange letter published on the Web site of the *Wichita Eagle*, Sanders's hometown newspaper. Instead of sending his all-important letter to the Detroit Lions staff, or William C. Ford, or even releasing it to the Detroit media or *The New York Times*, Sanders had given the *Eagle* its scoop of the decade:

> Shortly after the end of last season, I felt that I probably would not return for the 1999–2000 season. I also felt that I should take as much time as possible to sort through my feelings and make sure that my feelings were backed with conviction. Today, I officially declare my departure from the NFL.
>
> It was a wonderful experience to play in the NFL, and I have no regrets. I truly will miss playing for the Lions. I consider the Lions' players, coaches, staff, management, and fans my family. I leave on good terms with everyone in the organization. I have enjoyed playing for two great head coaches, Wayne Fontes and Bobby Ross, who are good coaches and leaders. I am not involved in a salary dispute of any kind. If I had played this season, I would have earned a more than satisfactory salary.
>
> The reason I am retiring is simple: My desire to exit the game is greater than my desire to remain in it. I have searched my heart through and through and feel comfortable with this decision.

I want to thank all the fans and media who made playing in the NFL such a wonderful experience. I have had the pleasure of meeting many of them. Although I was not able to honor many of your requests for autographs and interviews, it was not because I overlooked the importance of those who asked.

Finally, I want to thank my family and friends for their support and guidance. I wish my teammates, coaches, and the entire Lions organization all the best.

Say it isn't so!

That was the response of virtually all Lions fans and most other NFL fans around the country. Say it isn't so that the greatest running back of our time—perhaps the best of them all—was leaving the game at the age of 31. But that very number, those two short digits, were quite likely the reason for Sanders's retirement.

It is true that he was within striking distance of Walter Payton for the all-time yardage record, but he had never seemed highly motivated by that statistic. It is true that he would have made millions upon millions of dollars by staying in the game and that he could eventually have retired even richer than he was. But other than that, what was there to hold him in the game?

Sanders had seen two players—Mike Utley and Reggie Brown—carried off the field on stretchers. Utley was paralyzed for life, and Brown never returned to professional football. That was a serious consideration for someone like Sanders, who had enjoyed such great good fortune in rarely being injured over a 10-year NFL career. Though he never expressed it this way, Sanders may have also wished to go out on top. His 1997 performance, including 2,053 rushing yards, had been awe-inspiring, but his 1998 numbers were below par. More, he knew that almost every great running back has experienced a sudden drop-off in his numbers. Greats like Earl Campbell, Billy Sims, and even Gale Sayers (to whom

Sanders was often compared) had never been able to match their earlier numbers in later years, and it was not for want of trying. Perhaps Sanders made the best possible move, leaving the NFL when he was right at the top.

The response was mixed.

Some reporters reacted with a combination of anger and disbelief. How could Sanders walk out when he meant so much to the team, the fans, and the game?

Others applauded his independent spirit. Sanders, they said, was not ruled by public opinion or the commercial needs of the NFL. He was his own person.

This is what Peter King, longtime *Sports Illustrated* writer, had to say on the matter:

> A great talent has quit in his prime, and the game is diminished. But Sanders, walking the streets of London over the weekend, seemed perfectly comfortable with his decision. "I've talked with him every day since he left," [David] Ware [one of Barry's agents] said last Saturday night, "and it's obvious he has no regrets."

Jay Mariotti of the *Chicago Sun-Times* had this to offer:

> In the shadows you suspect there are other reasons. You do because the size of his heart has always over-whelmed his ego, assuming he really has one. During a somber, almost surreal news conference at the Pontiac Silverdome, it was suggested to Lions head coach Bobby Ross—blamed by Sanders' glib father, William, as the man who chased off his son—that [Walter] Payton's liver disease might have contributed to the retirement decision. Blessed with humility and perspective, Sanders is the sort of person who would have been painfully uncomfortable pursuing the all-time record if Payton were fighting for his life.

"With Barry, nothing would surprise me," said Ross, never veering off the high road. "He is that good a person."

Most fans—whether they lived in Detroit, Chicago, or anywhere else in the United States, genuinely mourned. Sanders had been one of the brightest lights of the NFL for a decade: Now he and his magic were gone.

WALKING AWAY: TWO STORIES

Throughout his 10-year NFL career, Barry Sanders had often been compared to the great running back Jim Brown, who had spent nine years with the Cleveland Browns. To many who had watched Brown play (including Sanders's father), he would always be No. 1, the greatest running back who ever lived. Regardless of where one comes down on the matter of "who's the greatest of them all," one can marvel at the synchronicity between the careers of the two men, and the manner of their departures from professional football.

In the summer of 1966, Brown was at the height of his earning power and professional prowess. He never earned anywhere near as much as Barry Sanders (1960s salaries were much lower than those of the 1990s), but he was well-off financially. Brown was in the early stages of what would become a prolific film career: He eventually starred in more than 30 movies and appeared in several television shows. In the summer of 1966, he was in London, doing early filming for *The Dirty Dozen*, which also starred Lee Marvin, Charles Bronson, and Telly Savalas. Brown would not be back in Cleveland in time for

SPECULATION

Fans, critics, and professional pundits continued to spin the story of Sanders's retirement. Two years after his abrupt departure from the NFL, speculation was that he would return to a new team with a new contract and a lot more money. But by the beginning of the 2001 season, this fervor had died out. Sanders was gone.

So were most of his teammates from the 1990s. Several had been traded away in the months prior to his departure.

training camp; upon learning this, the team owner issued an ultimatum: Return or be fired.

Brown chose to exit. His statement declared that he left the NFL with sadness but no regrets, and, when asked about it over the years, he always confirmed this feeling. Some of the brightness of 1960s football passed with his departure.

Thirty-three years later, right down to the month, Barry Sanders issued his statement to the *Wichita Eagle*, then flew to London for a vacation. Reporters got ahold of him there, but the media rush was not what Sanders would have experienced if he had stayed at home.

Was he angry? Had he left over money? Over hard feelings?

Sanders was, if anything, more cryptic than Brown. The reason was as he had given in the statement to his hometown newspaper: "My desire to exit the game is greater than my desire to remain in it."

Whatever their innermost reasons, Jim Brown and Barry Sanders exited the game in similar ways. Fans have lamented their departures ever since.

Herman Moore remained with the Lions until the end of 2001. He was then traded to the New York Giants, where he played for only one year. Moore ended his magnificent career with 670 receptions for 9,174 yards.

Johnnie Morton left the Lions the same year that Moore did, traded to the Kansas City Chiefs. He played three seasons with the Chiefs and one season with the San Francisco 49ers, retiring after the 2005 season. Over his career, Morton had amassed 624 receptions for 8,719 yards.

Kevin Glover, the longtime Detroit Lions center, was traded to the Seattle Seahawks at the end of 1997. He played there for two years, then retired after 15 years in the NFL.

Charlie Batch, the quarterback on whom so many hopes were pinned, was traded to the Pittsburgh Steelers at the end of 2001. His NFL career had not lived up to the promise with which it began.

Thurman Thomas, with whom Sanders had played at Oklahoma State, spent 13 seasons in the NFL, all but one of them with the Buffalo Bills. He retired in 2000, having compiled 12,074 rushing yards.

Rodney Peete, with whom Sanders had competed for the 1988 Heisman Trophy, played on six teams over 15 years in the NFL, before retiring in 2004.

Troy Aikman, another competitor for the 1988 Heisman, retired in 2000 after 12 years in the NFL, all of them with the Dallas Cowboys. His performance as quarterback had much to do with making the Cowboys the winningest team of the 1990s. Aikman led Dallas to three Super Bowl victories.

Deion Sanders retired in 2005, after 14 NFL seasons.

One could go on and on, citing the list of players with whom Sanders had played over a decade. Most of them were gone by 2005.

Everyone feels sadness at the end of an era. Sanders doubtless felt his share. But it had never been his style to talk about his feelings, and he left the NFL determined to begin a new life.

MARRIAGE AND FAMILY

Despite his good looks and enormous fame, Sanders had never been listed as Detroit's most eligible bachelor. He stayed home too much, was too content with leading a quiet life, for that. So it came as some surprise to learn that he was engaged and then married in 2000 to Lauren Campbell, a broadcaster with a Detroit news station.

The couple began a happy life together. They soon had a son, Nigel, who had a big brother in B.J. Sanders, the son Barry had had back in 1994. Barry's home life seemed complete, but there were still other challenges ahead.

RECONCILIATION

Over the years Sanders had done his best to play down, for public consumption, his on-again, off-again relationship with his father. William Sanders had been a scary figure in Barry's youth, the man who made him roof houses in 100-degree heat, and the father still loomed large during Barry's NFL career. William Sanders came to many of Barry's games, and his long, lean figure and the pipe he so frequently smoked were common sights to NFL broadcasters. People who pried beneath the appearance, however, eventually came to find that all was not well in this father-son relationship.

William Sanders had been furious with Barry for signing with Oklahoma State University way back in 1986. William Sanders had been displeased with his son for even considering staying at OSU for his senior year; in part, Barry had agreed to enter the NFL Draft because of his father's wishes.

Once he became an NFL star, earning lots of money, Barry was very good to his parents and his hometown; as mentioned earlier, he tithed (gave) 10 percent of his earnings to the Paradise Baptist Church. Barry bought a big, new house for his parents, ensuring that his father would not have to get up on hot roofs in the future. But no matter what Barry did for

In 2000, the year after his retirement, Barry Sanders married Lauren Campbell, a Detroit news broadcaster, and together they have a son, Nigel. Here, Lauren Sanders spoke in May 2003 at the forty-ninth annual induction ceremony for the Michigan Sports Hall of Fame. Lauren Sanders attended the ceremony on behalf of her husband.

his father, it did not seem good enough. In his autobiography *Now You See Him ...*, Barry later described one of the worst moments:

In the kitchen, in the home I'd bought for him in Wichita, he was bitterly explaining to me what I should be doing with my money. Much of that "advice" had to do with giving him more of it. Our relationship was at stake, he said, and before leaving the room, he approached me menacingly. That was the last time we would speak for a year.

William Sanders did not attend his son's wedding. The two did not become reconciled until after the birth of Barry and Lauren's son, Nigel. Barry expressed how that infant bridged some of the gap:

> Yet here we sat talking sports while he held my son. Who'd have thought that someone only twenty-one inches long could bridge all the miles of misunderstanding between my father and me? We obviously love each other, but in the preceding years and months, we collided like rams.

That was putting it mildly.

Relations between parents and children are usually complex. Parents want the best for their children, but sometimes they push them into doing things the children do not want. In the Sanderses' case, it is difficult to say which came first: football (or sports in general) and the desire to excel or the need to have a stable family foundation.

Fans who read about the father-son clashes were often surprised, for Barry was the mildest of men in person. But the quirks and strains in the relationship were evident when William Sanders gave a short speech on the occasion of his son's induction into the Pro Football Hall of Fame (he was accepted in 2004, the first year he was eligible).

William rose to speak. He felt the need to praise Jim Brown, he said, who was the greatest running back of them all. He

Barry Sanders and his father, William, acknowledged the crowd during the Pro Football Hall of Fame Festival Parade on August 7, 2004, in Canton, Ohio. The relationship between Barry and William Sanders has sometimes been a contentious one.

said he could not say very much about his son, because his son would soon speak for himself.

Reporters looked to Barry, who showed the same inscrutable face he had shown throughout his NFL career (the only exception had been his eyes, which would open very wide during a big run). There was no hint of disappointment; after all these years and all the fame and money that had come his way, Barry was still William Sanders's "kid," one who could only say, "Yes, Daddy."

When his own turn came, Barry was gracious to all, including his parents, on whom he lavished praise. Those watching

A CAREER IN RETROSPECT

Every great football player has his fans and his detractors: It goes with the territory. Throughout his 10-year NFL career, Barry Sanders heard more from the former than the latter, but soon after he retired, the naysayers and doubters re-emerged. Was he truly as great as people claimed?

One way to run a comparison is between the greatest days of the greatest running backs. Sanders seemed, in general, to have his best rushing days against the Tampa Bay Buccaneers; there was the hilarious "Sock Hop" of 1994 and the 1997 afternoon in which he had two rushing touchdowns, both of 80 yards or more. He gained 237 yards on his best NFL day.

Sanders's closest competitors were running greats O.J. Simpson of the Buffalo Bills and Walter Payton of the Chicago Bears. For years, until 2000, Payton had the all-time best rushing day, with 275 yards against the Minnesota Vikings on November 20, 1977. Simpson had the two next-highest rushing days, with 273 yards against the Detroit Lions on November 25, 1976 (the Thanksgiving Day game) and 250 yards against the New England Patriots on September 16, 1973.

With the exception of Simpson's 250-yard day, almost all of the truly "big" rushing days seem to come late in the season, often in November. Is this merely a coincidence? Or does it sometimes take that long for a running back to find his timing in a 14-game or 16-game season?

Many who watched Sanders at his best thought he was the best running back of them all, but it must be conceded that both Payton and Simpson rushed in what were consistently more difficult conditions; the Chicago Bears and the Buffalo Bills played their home games outdoors, not in the climate-

(continues)

(continued)

controlled atmosphere of the Silverdome. And finally, it must be said that Sanders was not a big contributor in postseason games. He certainly tried, rushing time and again against the Washington Redskins, the Green Bay Packers, the Philadelphia Eagles, and the Tampa Bay Buccaneers, but his postseason performances were generally well below his regular-season ones.

Was Sanders "the best" runner of the 1990s? Most commentators think so. Will anyone rush like that again? Let us hope so, for the fans, the sport, and the NFL.

that day had it confirmed in their minds that here was a man of greatness: one who excelled but did not lose his original spirit. Before long it was over, and Barry was one of the newest members of the Pro Football Hall of Fame (fellow inductees that year were Broncos quarterback John Elway, Vikings defensive end Carl Eller, and offensive tackle Bob "Boomer" Brown).

WRAPPING UP

Competition and comparison are two separate things. People compete all the time, but comparisons are difficult to make because it is so rare that the playing field (whether figurative or literal) is truly a level one. No story of Barry Sanders would be complete without a host of comparisons, however, so these are offered in the spirit of fun and adventure:

- Sanders was probably the fastest man ever to run in the NFL.

The Detroit Lions honored Barry Sanders on December 23, 2007, during halftime of their game with the Kansas City Chiefs. The ceremony marked the tenth anniversary of the season in which Sanders rushed for 2,053 yards.

- He was certainly among the quickest, but his quickness was not quite as great as his speed.
- Sanders invented all sorts of new moves, such as the 360-degree turn that left defenders gasping.
- He was fun to watch.

In his 10-year NFL career, Sanders ran 3,062 times and gained 15,269 yards, for a per-rush average of 5.0 yards. He scored 99 rushing touchdowns. It is hard to say which year was his "best," but most commentators look to 1997, the season in which he rushed 335 times for 2,053 yards, or an average of 6.1 yards per carry.

Soon after Sanders left the NFL, one other great running back—Emmitt Smith—passed Sanders and then Walter Payton on the all-time list of yards gained. Sanders remains in third place overall.

One may ask: What if he had stayed five more years? How many yards might he have gained? Sadly, these efforts are usually futile. They overlook the essential importance of youth in the career of a running back; a premier NFL athlete only has a few years of greatness before time, effort, and chance begin to catch up. Sanders went out at the top, and there he remains in the minds of his many devoted fans.

And so we are left with the man, the little boy from Wichita who ran the ball because he loved doing so. The little boy became the quiet, respectful man, beloved by his teammates and admired by peers in the game. While no one is perfect—and no life is without its blemishes—we can safely say that Barry Sanders has carried himself with style, class, and a refreshing lack of self-importance, all of which made him even greater in the eyes of those who watched the game.

STATISTICS

BARRY SANDERS
Position: Running back

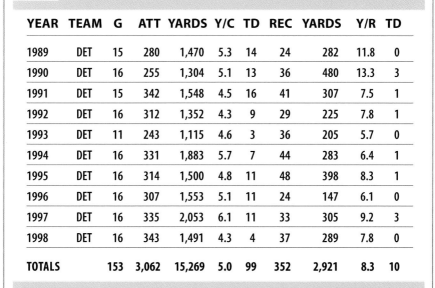

FULL NAME: **Barry David Sanders**
BORN: **July 16, 1968,
Wichita, Kansas**
HEIGHT: **5'8"**
WEIGHT: **200 lbs.**

COLLEGE: **Oklahoma
State University**
TEAMS: **Detroit Lions
(1989–1998)**

YEAR	TEAM	G	ATT	YARDS	Y/C	TD	REC	YARDS	Y/R	TD
1989	DET	15	280	1,470	5.3	14	24	282	11.8	0
1990	DET	16	255	1,304	5.1	13	36	480	13.3	3
1991	DET	15	342	1,548	4.5	16	41	307	7.5	1
1992	DET	16	312	1,352	4.3	9	29	225	7.8	1
1993	DET	11	243	1,115	4.6	3	36	205	5.7	0
1994	DET	16	331	1,883	5.7	7	44	283	6.4	1
1995	DET	16	314	1,500	4.8	11	48	398	8.3	1
1996	DET	16	307	1,553	5.1	11	24	147	6.1	0
1997	DET	16	335	2,053	6.1	11	33	305	9.2	3
1998	DET	16	343	1,491	4.3	4	37	289	7.8	0
TOTALS		**153**	**3,062**	**15,269**	**5.0**	**99**	**352**	**2,921**	**8.3**	**10**

CHRONOLOGY

1934   Portsmouth (Ohio) Spartans move to Detroit and are renamed the Detroit Lions.

1950s   The Lions are one of the powerhouses in professional football.

1968   Barry Sanders is born on July 16 in Wichita, Kansas.

1975   The Detroit Lions move to the new Silverdome.

1986   Barry enters Oklahoma State University.

1986–1987   Plays behind Thurman Thomas at OSU.

1988   In junior season, sets 25 NCAA records, including most rushing yards in a season (2,628) and most touchdowns (39).
Wins the Heisman Trophy.

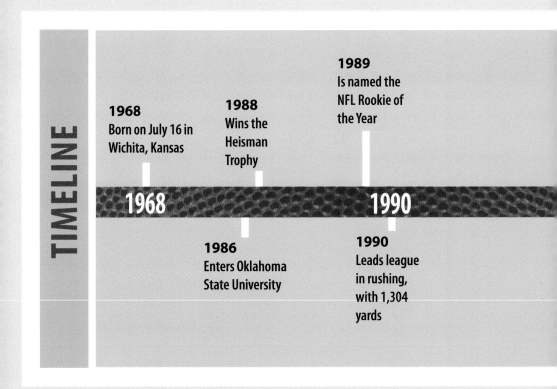

TIMELINE

1968
Born on July 16 in Wichita, Kansas

1988
Wins the Heisman Trophy

1989
Is named the NFL Rookie of the Year

1986
Enters Oklahoma State University

1990
Leads league in rushing, with 1,304 yards

1968   1990

1989   Is drafted by the Detroit Lions with the No. 3 pick in the first round.
Breaks the Lions' rookie rushing record, with 1,470 yards.
Is named the NFL Rookie of the Year.

1990   Leads the NFL in rushing, with 1,304 yards.

1991   Barry's sister Nancy dies of cancer.
Lions teammate Mike Utley is paralyzed after suffering a spinal-cord injury during a game.
The Lions go 12–4 and make the playoffs; they defeat Dallas 38-6 in a divisional playoff game but lose to Washington 41-10 in the NFC Championship Game.

1992   Lions finish 5–11.

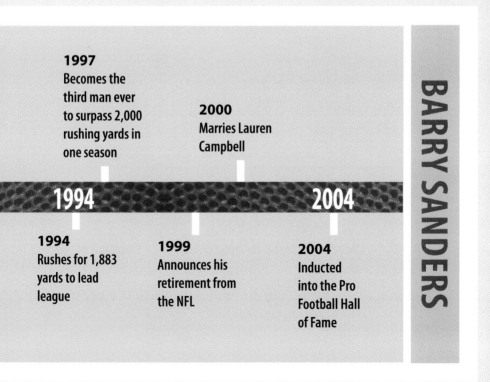

1997
Becomes the third man ever to surpass 2,000 rushing yards in one season

2000
Marries Lauren Campbell

1994

2004

1994
Rushes for 1,883 yards to lead league

1999
Announces his retirement from the NFL

2004
Inducted into the Pro Football Hall of Fame

BARRY SANDERS

1993	Lions finish 10–6; lose to Green Bay 28-24 in a wild-card playoff game.
1994	Leads the league in rushing, with 1,883 yards. Lions finish 9–7; again lose to Green Bay in the playoffs 16-12.
1995	Lions finish 10–6; again lose in the first round of the playoffs, this time by 58-37 to the Philadelphia Eagles.
1996	Leads the NFL in rushing with 1,553 yards. Lions finish 5–11; coach Wayne Fontes is fired.
1997	Bobby Ross becomes the new Lions head coach. Sanders has a lackluster first two games of season; he then goes on a tear of 14 consecutive games with 100 rushing yards or more. Becomes the third man ever to surpass 2,000 rushing yards in one season, finishing with a league-leading 2,053 yards. Lions finish 9–7; lose to Tampa Bay 20-10 in a wild-card playoff game.
1998	Lions finish 5–11.
1999	Just before training camp, Sanders announces his retirement from the NFL.
2000	Marries Lauren Campbell.
2003	Sanders's autobiography, co-written with Mark E. McCormick, is published. Sanders is inducted into the College Football Hall of Fame.
2004	Is inducted into the Pro Football Hall of Fame in his first year of eligibility.

GLOSSARY

bye week   A week in which a team does not play.

carry   The act of running with the ball.

center   A player position on offense. The center snaps the ball.

cornerback   A defensive back who lines up near the line of scrimmage across from a wide receiver. The cornerback's primary job is to disrupt passing routes, to defend against short and medium passes, and to contain the rusher on rushing plays.

draft   The selection of collegiate players for entrance into the National Football League. Typically, the team with the worst record in the previous season picks first in the draft.

end zone   The area between the end line and the goal line, bounded by the sidelines.

field goal   A scoring play of three points made by kicking the ball through the goalposts in the opponent's end zone.

first down   The first of a set of four downs. Usually, a team that has a first down needs to advance the ball 10 yards to receive another first down, but penalties or field position (i.e. less than 10 yards from the opposing end zone) can affect this.

fourth down   The final of a set of four downs. Unless a first down is achieved or a penalty forces a replay of the down, the team will lose control of the ball after this play. If a team does not think it can get a first down, it will often punt on fourth down or attempt a field goal if close enough to do so.

fumble   When any offensive player loses possession of the ball before the play is blown dead.

guard   A member of the offensive line. There are two guards, and they line up on either side of the center.

Heisman Trophy   An award presented annually to the most outstanding player in Division I-A college football.

hip pointer   A deep bruise to the hip bone or to the muscles attached to it.

interception   A pass that is caught by a defensive player, giving his team the ball.

kickoff   A kick that puts the ball into play at the start of the first and third quarters and after every touchdown and field goal.

linebacker   A player position on defense. Linebackers typically play one to six yards behind the defensive linemen. Most defenses use either three or four linebackers.

line of scrimmage   The imaginary line that stretches across the field and separates the two teams before the snap; before a play, teams line up on either side of the line of scrimmage.

offensive line   The offensive players who line up on the line of scrimmage. Their primary job is to block the defensive players.

Pro Bowl   The all-star game of the NFL, played a week after the Super Bowl. Players are voted to the Pro Bowl by coaches, fellow players, and fans. Each group's ballots count for one-third of the vote.

quarterback   The offensive player who receives the ball from the center at the start of each play. The quarterback will hand off the ball, pass the ball, or run it himself.

rookie   A player in his first year as a professional.

running back   An offensive player who runs with the football; also known as a tailback, halfback, or fullback.

run and shoot offense   An offensive philosophy designed to force the defense to show its hand before the ball is snapped. This is done by splitting receivers and sending them in motion. Receivers run patterns based on the play of the defenders rather than a predetermined route.

rush   A running play; also, an attempt to tackle or hurry a player before he can make a pass or kick the ball.

safety   A defensive player who lines up in the secondary but often deeper than the cornerbacks. A safety is also a two-point score that occurs by downing an opposing ball carrier in his own end zone.

salary cap   The limit that a team can spend on players' salaries in a given year.

signing bonus   An amount of money a player receives just to sign with a team.

tackle   The act of forcing a ball carrier to the ground; also, a player position on the offensive or defensive line.

touchdown   A play worth six points in which any part of the ball while legally in the possession of a player crosses the plane of the opponent's goal line. A touchdown allows the team a chance for one extra point by kicking the ball or a two-point conversion by running or passing the ball into the end zone.

wide receiver   A player position on offense. He is split wide (usually about 10 yards) from the formation and plays on the line of scrimmage as a split end or one yard off as a flanker.

wingback   A running back used in a wing formation. The back lines up just outside the tight end and one yard off the line of scrimmage.

wild card   The two playoff spots given to the two non-division-winning teams that have the best records in the conference.

yard   One yard of linear distance in the direction of one of the two goals. A field is 100 yards. Typically, a team is required to advance at least 10 yards to get a new set of downs.

BIBLIOGRAPHY

BOOKS

Boyles, Bob, and Paul Guido. *50 Years of College Football: A Modern History of America's Most Colorful Sport.* New York: Skyhorse Publishing, 2007.

Knapp, Ron. *Sports Great Barry Sanders.* Berkeley Heights, N.J.: Enslow Publishers Inc., 1999.

Frisch, Aaron. *Detroit Lions.* Mankato, Minn.: Creative Education, 2005.

Gay, Timothy, Ph.D. *The Physics of Football: Discover the Science of Bone-Crushing Hits, Soaring Fields Goals, and Awe-Inspiring Passes.* New York: HarperCollins, 2005.

MacCambridge, Michael. *ESPN College Football Encyclopedia.* New York: ESPN Books, 2005.

MacCambridge, Michael. *America's Game: The Epic Story of How Pro Football Captured a Nation.* New York: Random House, 2004.

Rand, Jonathan. *Run It! And Let's Get the Hell Out of Here!: The 100 Best Plays in Pro Football History.* Guilford, Conn.: Globe Pequot Press, 2007.

Sanders, Barry, with Mark E. McCormick. *Barry Sanders: Now You See Him…* Cincinnati, Ohio: Emmis Books, 2003.

Sanders, Charlie, with Larry Paladino. *Tales from the Detroit Lions.* Champaign, Ill.: Sports Publishing LLC, 2005.

Schumer, Barry, *"I Don't Believe It!": Memories of a Detroit Lions Fan.* Bloomington, Ind.: AuthorHouse, 2006.

ARTICLES

Anderson, Dave. "Minus 1: New Number for Barry Sanders." *The New York Times,* January 1, 1995.

George, Thomas. "Favre Saves Day in Final Minute." *The New York Times,* January 9, 1994.

———. "Lions Out of Bounds and Out of Playoffs." *The New York Times,* January 1, 1995.

———. "Bucs' Playoff Novices Check Sanders and Deck the Lions." *The New York Times*, December 29, 1997.

———. "An Injury Puts Chill in Lions." *The New York Times*, December 29, 1997.

Hinton, Ed. "Cut and Run: The Wizardry of Detroit's Barry Sanders Has NFL Defenses Wondering How in the World to Stop Him." *Sports Illustrated*, December 5, 1994.

King, Peter. "Why Barry Bolted: The Inside Story." *Sports Illustrated*, August 9, 1999.

Mariotti, Jay. "Say Bye to Barry: Classy Sanders Has His Reasons." *Chicago Sun-Times*, July 29, 1999.

Montville, Leigh. "Pigskin on Turkey Day." *Sports Illustrated*, extra issue, Fall 1995.

Murphy, Austin. "A Lamb Among Lions." *Sports Illustrated*, September 10, 1990.

Silver, Michael. "Wild Weekend." *Sports Illustrated*, January 8, 1996.

Smith, Timothy W. "Inspired by a Foolhardy Detroit Guarantee, Eagles Light Up Scoreboard." *The New York Times*, December 31, 1995.

Telander, Rick. "Big Hand for a Quiet Man." *Sports Illustrated*, December 12, 1988.

Zimmerman, Paul. "Lion King: Barry Sanders Is Running Circles Around NFL Defenses with an Electrifying Style Unlike Anything the League Has Seen." *Sports Illustrated*, December 8, 1997.

FILMS (VHS OR DVD)

Barry! NFL Films, 1995

Foundation for the Future, highlights of the 1989 Detroit Lions, NFL Films.

One Small Step, highlights of the 1997 Detroit Lions, NFL Films.

Roaring Ahead, highlights of the 1998 Detroit Lions, NFL Films.

Thumbs Up, highlights of the 1991 Detroit Lions, NFL Films.

FURTHER READING

BOOKS

Bass, Tom. *The New Coach's Guide to Youth Football Skills and Drills*. New York: McGraw-Hill, 2005.

Long, Howie and John Czarnecki. *Football for Dummies*. New York: John Wiley and Sons, 2007.

McDonough, Will. *The NFL Century: The Complete Story of the National Football League, 1920–2000*. New York: Smithmark, 1999.

Palmer, Pete, et al. *The ESPN Pro Football Encyclopedia*. New York: Sterling Publishing, 2007.

2007 NFL Record & Fact Book. New York: National Football League, 2007.

WEB SITES

Barry Sanders: Pro Football Hall of Fame
http://www.profootballhof.com/hof/member.jsp?PLAYER_ID=187

The Lions Video Vault
http://www.detroitlions.com/document_display.cfm?document_id=320371

The NFL on ESPN.com
http://sports-ak.espn.go.com/nfl/index

The Official Site of the National Football League
http://www.nfl.com

The Official Web Site of Barry Sanders
http://barrysanders.com/

The Official Web Site of the Detroit Lions
http://www.detroitlions.com/

Pro Football Reference
http://www.pro-football-reference.com

Sporting News: Barry Sanders
http://www.sportingnews.com/archives/sanders/

PICTURE CREDITS

INDEX

ABOUT THE AUTHOR

SAMUEL WILLARD CROMPTON grew up playing tennis rather than football, but he is very aware of the level of competitiveness that characterizes both sports. A part-time professor of history, at Westfield State College and Holyoke Community College, he is also a full-time writer. Working from his home in the scenic Berkshire Hills of western Massachusetts, he has written many books with Chelsea House, including biographies of John Elway and Peyton Manning. Crompton is a major contributor to the 24-volume *American National Biography* and wrote most of the tennis entries for the two-volume *Scribner's Encyclopedia of American Lives*, the sports edition.